SILENT PRAIRIE

Silent Prairie

Leah L. P. Hiebert

Illustrated by
Sarah Hiebert Watkins

VANTAGE PRESS
New York

Published by Vantage Press, Inc.
516 West 34th Street, New York, New York 10001

Manufactured in the United States of America
ISBN: 0-533-09364-3

Library of Congress Catalog Card No.: 90-91402

1 2 3 4 5 6 7 8 9 0

To my four granddaughters, for their inspiring and encouraging words

Contents

Foreword

Vitality and optimism, humor and charm, determination and gentleness, these are some of the qualities that characterize Leah Penner Hiebert.

It has been my privilege to be her friend for almost ten years, ever since we met at one of the meetings of The Shenandoah Valley Artists Association. Different in ethnic, cultural, and religious backgrounds, Leah and I have found common grounds in our devotion to family, love of the arts, the simple life of our childhood, and the travels of military wives across the continents. And we are both Americans by choice!

Leah's recounting of her "prairie days" experiences or her "fifty journeys" has always fascinated me. Her ability to recall and describe events that took place so long ago is truly remarkable. But she has been blessed with other talents, too. Her success with painting and sculpture is well documented in many magazine and newspaper articles about her exhibits in the United States, Europe and Japan. There is evidence of her prolific artistry in her home, from a high- and low-relief of seven astronauts to a bronze of President Kennedy; from portraits of her husband and grandchildren to colorful landscapes.

A heart patient for thirty-five years, Leah is fiercely independent. Her two sons would like for her to move in with them or, at least, closer; she prefers to visit them occasionally and live alone in the modest home she shared with Dr. Hiebert after his retirement as a chaplain in the U.S. Army. Once a week a woman does the cleaning and takes her shopping; neighbors and friends often stop by to say hello; Lucy, her pet cockatiel, is never too far. The grounds surrounding the house abound with flowers and fruits, reflecting her careful planning, her commitment, and her caring.

The nostalgia for the ways of a pristine life has not stopped Leah from being a thoroughly modern woman. She is up to date on issues, mores, and styles; therefore, she is the perfect confidante and counselor of her four granddaughters. She gives them credit for encouraging her to write. Sarah Hiebert Watkins, who has obviously inherited her grandmother's artistic talents, has designed the illustrations for *Silent Prairie*.

It may seem a paradox, but the "secret" of Leah's successful life is no secret at all. Her activities keep her young in spirit and give her strength. As I approach my senior years, whenever I worry about the autumn of my life, I think of Leah Penner Hiebert and feel rejuvenated.

Nella Danese Weir
Stephens City, Virginia

Preface

My book is a semi-biographical account of memories during my childhood while living in the far northwestern prairies of Canada beginning with the year of 1897 until 1923. The stories that happened prior to my earliest memory were repeated to me many times by my relatives. For the sake of posterity, I am telling it as I remember it happening. The episodes, dates, and places are all true; some names have been changed.

It is about actual people who lived through those years and who have all gone beyond by now.

My childhood days until twelve years of age were normal even with the hardships and the violent climate. At the age of twelve my dream castles all toppled down. Then a Cinderella type of life had to be endured for several years.

During my teenage days from the age of fourteen until twenty in California, I had to work to support my mother. At the same time, I took my high school courses in my hours off from work.

I had to adjust to many changes as there was never any one way of living. I loved life and always reached for new horizons, but wanted life to love me back.

I was too often accused of laughing too much, as I always saw some silver lining around the dark clouds, and expected to work hard to find a rainbow at some new place. The people would often tease and laugh at me because of my accent, as I was brought up with the Dutch, German, and the old British languages before I came to America.

When twenty years old, while in college, I discovered my talent as an artist in painting and sculpturing. After that I forgot all about my nurse's training.

In 1930 I was married to a young clergy student. I was fascinated with his fervor in his religious belief and I wanted his kind of life.

Thereafter, my life was very active as a minister's wife, having two sons, moving and living in fifty different places in the fifty years of my marriage. I never neglected my artistic endeavors, taking art courses wherever we lived, joining art groups and exhibiting my paintings and sculptures, ending up teaching art in elementary schools and then college. I rented an in-town studio to teach all ages.

After our fiftieth wedding anniversary in 1980 I wrote and published a book, titled *Fifty Journeys*, about the fifty places we lived across the U.S.A. and crossing both oceans four times.

During World War II my husband joined the army as a chaplain. He was three years at the battlefront in Europe, was wounded, and, after serving twenty years in the army, was promoted to Colonel when he retired. Mr. Hiebert attended college and seminary school, earning his Th.D. and Ph.D.

My sons, Adoniram and Dennis, are both mechanical engineers and they are now designing automatic robots.

My sons have given me five grandchildren and I also have two great-grandchildren.

My husband died two years ago. His illness was stomach cancer; three years of agonizing pain. I took care of him every hour of the day.

I have had three heart failure attacks due to past rheumatic fever.

I now live alone in a country cottage and still enjoy life. To me aging is a joy. I hope to live another ten years, until 90 years old.

I am a late bloomer with my writings and do not feel I am

a good writer, but I do feel I have something to tell about life of the past to the modern generation.

My granddaughters inspired me to write this book, always asking for stories of my life as a child. I decided others might enjoy reading about the childhood life in the wilderness in the early 1900s.

My message is that one can find pleasure and happiness even in the frontier life. The children have to invent their own entertainment and mischief, never saying "I cannot" until you have tried it.

I admit that I have achieved many things and have not stopped planning ahead. At eighty-one years of age I plan to write three more books. It takes me about two years to write a book.

Acknowledgments

Many thanks for typing and helping with many things to Nella, Edna, Carol, Dennis and Adoniram.

To Mary Eden for editing.

My appreciation to my neighbors for their patience in looking after my health.

I especially appreciate all the information on and description of my father that my Uncle Jake in Canada revealed to me.

SILENT PRAIRIE

Cornelious Ben Piner, age 18 (Born 1884—Died 1912)

Chapter I

A Strong Desire

"I must go!" young Cornelious shouted in the midst of a sun-drenched wheat field, thinking he was alone.

A soft voice behind him said, "You must go where?" It was Uncle Abe.

Recovering from being startled, Cornelious bashfully answered, "Westward to cultivate the prairie."

"That is a childish dream; first grow up," retorted the older man.

Angered, the young man kicked at sheaves standing against each other. "I am sixteen, doing a man's work on this farm."

"A male becomes a man at twenty-one according to the law of this land." Uncle Abe had a loud voice when irritated.

Cornelious came back with a high-pitched voice: "You told me when I turned sixteen that I was old enough to stop school and work on this farm, and I have done a good job. I have taken all responsibility like a man."

Whenever Cornelious mentioned to anyone his dream to go west, he always heard: "Wait until you are eighteen." He was generally a happy person with a big smile even when things did not go well, but when he couldn't get anyone to listen to him he would feel frustrated.

He missed his father very much. They had talked about the Far West with great enthusiasm. Several times his father had

1

said, "My son, whatever your plans are for your future, never give up."

Cornelious's father, Cornelious Piner, Sr., had died quietly in his sleep while taking a noonday nap. It had been a hot day, and he was feeling tired after a hard morning out in the field.

Home was a large farm near a village called Steinback about ten miles from Winnipeg, Manitoba. The people residing in this area were mostly the Belgium Dutch-speaking people. Some came from Germany, Austria, Sweden, and Russia. The majority were Mennonites in religion, very strong in discipline and very clannish. The relatives stayed together. Leaving home for good was the wrong thing to do, and often the young men who left would be banned from the congregation.

Cornelious was fourteen years old when his father died, and his real mother had died when he was very young.

His Uncle Abe was the older brother of his father who took charge of the farm until the three young brothers would take over. Uncle Abe was a big man, heavyset, with a headful of reddish blond hair and a large beard to match. In fact, the whole family looked like Swedes, not Germans. They all had ruddy complexions and blue-gray eyes.

Uncle Abe was rigid in manners and strong in principles and the leader of the clan. Cornelious's father had been the jolly one, always free with his laughter.

Cornelious had this strong, youthful urge for adventure and was determined to follow his dream. He would hang around the general merchant stores waiting for the fur traders to come back from the western hunting grounds and ask these men hundreds of questions. Cornelious would take his horse and ride in to Winnipeg to get information and maps from the Canadian government land office. There he was told that the new provinces of Alberta and Saskatchewan were offering free homesteads to young men. But these provinces had not yet been officially mapped out. In a few more years the railroad would be extended to the western area, which would make traveling faster.

Cornelious was handsome and tall, with an ever-present friendly smile. It was easy to respond to his questions. On his eighteenth birthday he looked up his best friend among the fur traders. Cornelious pulled out his handmade map and the list of his plans and started to inquire on all the details, insisting he would ride horseback alone with a packhorse. Cornelious got help finding a strong riding horse and a dependable packhorse to carry his supplies.

First on the list were some sacks of oats in case the horses could not find enough grass, cans for extra water, and, wrapped in burlap, lightweight saddles. The horses' feet had to be shod. The food for himself was dried meat, called jerky, dried apples, and dried wheat kernels. His bedding had to be of goose feathers and sheep wool. His clothing of a heavy long sheepskin coat, chaparajos, heavy furlike leggings to wrap around his legs for when he was on horseback, and a wide-brimmed felt hat to protect him from the rain and wind. The chaparajos had the hair on the inside while the leather was on the outside to keep the legs dry and warm. He also needed a .30 caliber deer rifle to hunt rabbit and fowl and a bottle of turpentine for medication. He did not believe in using a horse whip or spurs to encourage his horses.

On January 19, 1902, Cornelious came into the house stomping the snow off his boots from shoveling a path to the barn. The smell of fresh baked bread made his heart melt.

The family sitting around the dining table arose and sang out, "Happy birthday, Cornie!" This had never happened in this home before.

He asked, "How come?"

His stepmother, whom he called Mother, patted his back and softly said, "You have been saying that at eighteen you would leave for the West; we want you to remember this occasion—happy eighteenth birthday."

Mother continued talking. "We have extra news today. Your brother David sent a message to Uncle Abe that he reached Minnesota with the emigrants. He was continuing, going westward toward the Pacific Ocean to Oregon."

Brother David was a few years older then Cornelious. He always made it clear that he was not going to be a farmer. This was the first message they had received since he left six months ago.

Cornelious remarked, "Thank you all for a wonderful birthday. I shall leave in March, as soon as the snow goes away. Uncle Abe and Brother Abe will take care of this farm."

Mother answered with a sad expression, "Your brother Abe does not show any interest in the farm stock nor the work."

The family started to separate. Cornelious called out, "From now on I want to be called by my middle name! I shall answer to Ben, not Cornelious!"

Ben left the village in the early morning of April 13, 1902, several burlap sacks holding up his supplies all tied on the packhorse's saddle, rolls of blankets and his overcoat wrapped onto the back of his riding horse.

Chapter II

A Wild Adventure

On this beautiful spring day, Ben rode down the street. His neighbors and relatives came to the edge of the road to wish him luck, as if they did not expect to see him again. They all called out, "Good-bye Ben!" as the word of his new name had spread. He himself had no idea when he would be back home again. His large-brimmed hat shielded his eyes from the sun, as it shielded his tears from the onlookers. He did not know what he would face, as he had not been more than fifteen miles out into the country before.

He could feel the ground under the grass was still damp and soggy from the melted snow. He had left his family a partial plan of his trip. He would try to reach the edge of the prairie in about ten days, then he would be entering Saskatchewan.

He calmed down by the noon hour. The birds greeted him all around. The rabbits hopped out and faced him as if accepting him into their world.

The trees started to show light-colored green foliage. Spring was popping out all over. He stopped at noon hour to eat the sandwich his stepmother had tucked into his pocket. Around his waist was a wide, soft leather belt with holes from which to hang his two folding knives, and Grandfather's large pocketwatch, but he had no calendar and no compass.

He had sketched out a partial map. He was told to try to follow the small streams but stay south of the large lakes. His own motto was to follow the sun and keep his mind geared toward the north. Edmonton, Alberta was his destination, or when he could see the Rocky Mountains. In his jacket pockets he had several small pads and pencils to write his daily diary. For another pastime he had two very small books of poetry, one in English, another in Dutch, a history book of Canada, and a German Bible. His family language was called Low Dutch from an area near the Belgian border. It was a mixture of Holland-Dutch and Belgium-Dutch, and therefore had no written books. It was a constant choice to read the Dutch or the German and the English.

Day in, day out this lonely trail kept him busy. He did not keep the diary of his first ten days.

*　　*　　*

DIARY—APRIL 23, 1902, EARLY MORNING

I made it; this is my tenth day, and I see the prairies. It's so flat, seeing as far as my eyes can see, tan-colored grass, deep grass folded over into waves. The sun is very bright. There are no shadows, no trees, no post nor a hill to a make a shadow. It looks like God sliced from the flat prairie all the green hills and trees and bushes with a knife. I must be in that new province called Saskatchewan, as the fur traders called it, "where the buffalo and the Indians roam free from all worries." I am resting for the rest of the day. I have relieved the horses of their weights.

In my diary I have made a mark on each sunset, and this is the tenth sunset, just as I had planned. I figured I did 250 miles. Each day I changed the horses from a walk to a trot and then short gallops. I walked fast for several miles each day. I have checked and cleaned the horses' hooves, and now they are both rolling over on the cool grass. Every evening I have given

First sight of the prairie—April 23, 1902

the horses' back and legs a rubdown; tonight I will not need to, as they are stretching out all their limbs.

It is so silent, I am afraid to even give a whistle; it might crack the air. The birds have gone to roost in the trees and bushes in the green area.

The sky is so open, no clouds in sight. I am so excited, I feel no sleep coming tonight.

APRIL 24, MORNING

The silence allowed me to sleep until the sun hit my face. A breakfast of chewy jerky and one hard biscuit. I cannot find a sign of anyone or anything having walked in this grass; all I can do is follow the sun for the day.

The horses hesitate to step on the waves of long grass. I know their shod hooves will protect their feet from the hard blades of grass.

NOON HOUR

I had to lead them for a few miles until we hit on some short grass where the ground was hard; then I rode fast to make up for lost time. The horses hesitate to walk on the long grass folded over in waves; it feels like walking on a feather bed.

APRIL 25

This is my third day on this eternal grassland as if there is no end to it, nothing living here. The horses refuse to chew on the tough, long grass; for the first time I gave them some grain. I have found no sign of water, and I gave the horses a few swallows of the water I had in the tin cans. I dug small holes as I went along so that I will know when I am walking in circles. I feel lost. I try to keep going what I think is northwest.

I promised myself to cook some of the rolled oats and must try the long grass as a fire. There has not been much wind yet.

APRIL 26

Early morning, the wind started to blow. I really felt the chill, and I tried to make a shelter out of burlap and canvass.

I was eating the leftover cooked oats when I heard a slight swishing in the grass. It crawled across my boot. "Good morning to you; it's good to see some living thing," I said; then another snake followed it, going toward the horses. They both jumped two feet on seeing the snakes. The packhorse is a very tranquil animal; she likes me to talk to her. The horses like it when I talk and sing to them; their ears twitch with the rhythm. Just to hear some voice, I often talk until my voice gives out.

Those snakes make me think. *They like to be near water. Maybe I am getting close to a creek.* The sun is out as bright as ever, and I have not seen a cloud yet. I feel the open space of freedom.

APRIL 27

Last night I had a most happy experience. I heard a coyote in the distance; there is some life after all. I have memorized half the Bible in all three languages. The Holland-Dutch is hardest to understand.

We hit another area of low grass, and there I found a buffalo chip. It must be the buffalo that eat this grass down.

Suddenly the horses lifted their heads and sniffed and I knew they smelled water; I had no more problem with the slow walk with them.

The wind is still very sharp; at times my arms get very numb from the cold. All I can hear is the swish of the wind. The open sky above is all around me. I try to persuade myself that I will make it. It's the loneliness and silence that is unusual. My fur trader friend warned me that the loneliness would be the hardest thing, telling me, "You will feel at times you are the only person alive in the world."

I still can hear the remarks of the relatives: "It's only for mature, strong-willed men"; "the Indians will make your end"; "it's for fearless men, not boys."

APRIL 28

The horses are still raring to go, so there must be water someplace near. This is my fifteenth day of having not seen another person. If I could find a wagon trail or a buffalo path I would be so very happy to know there had been a living thing before me.

Chapter III

Indians

APRIL 28, LATER

I looked down and there I saw a wide path. It did not look like a wagon trail, but something solid was being slid along—following tracks of hoofprints. I followed it until almost dark. The wind stopped and it turned warmer; spring has a way of coming in very quietly and softly tapping your shoulder with a whisper.

I heard a noise so I followed it, and suddenly I found myself in the middle of an Indian camp. There were several tepees with big pieces of leather draped around them.

Three young boys came running toward me smiling, dressed comfortably, and greeting me with words I could not understand with a feeling of meeting friends. I slid off my horse; the boys reached for the packhorse, starting to unstrap my belongings. I held them off as, I felt they might take it all. I looked up at a middle-aged man with an Indian blanket covering a regular business suit. He stretched out his hand and spoke in English: "Welcome, friend." I was still watching the boys fussing with my supplies. The man called to the boys. To me he said, "The boys will lead your horses to water; they were looking to see if you carried fresh furs." Then I remembered the fur traders' saying, "The Indians hate fur traders, feeling that we intrude on their livelihood."

"Come join us by the fire for some food," said the Indian in a soft voice.

Several women stood up with outstretched welcoming gestures. I sat beside the father and husband, as he seemed to be. More children brought armfuls of long grass, putting them beside the fire. Whatever was cooking smelled like roast beef. He started to ask me questions with slow, hesitant words, as if he had to think out the next word. "Your horses are tired-looking; how far have you come?"

I told him that this was my eighteenth day of riding. He walked over to my horses, slid his hands around their legs, and looked at their hooves.

He came back saying, "The condition of a man's horse proves the man. Their steel shoes have kept your horses in such good condition."

The cooked meat was cut off in small pieces and passed around with small bone spears.

"You are eating buffalo meat. Very good, yes?" he asked.

As I was trying to wipe my greasy hands, he said, "No, no, rub it into your hands, good for skin."

I asked him many questions. They had traveled from Newfoundland, he said. "We found the country in the East getting too populated, not enough food and open spaces for the Indians. We are called the Cree Indians and are looking for the Saskatoon Indians in Saskatchewan. Our language is called Ojibway. Further west are the Chippewa, an Indian part of the Algonquin-speaking tribe."

I was invited to sleep in the men's tepee.

APRIL 29

It was warm in the tepee, but outside it was bitterly cold. I asked my host if I could stay with them awhile, saying, "I will be glad to help or pay for my time here."

He was slow in responding, as if he was thinking, then said, "You may stay and travel with us for two weeks, if you will give my children some English lessons. Have a class with them two hours a day." He pulled out a pocketwatch showing the time.

Every day they all got up with the sun. Eight children gathered around me, looking up at me with an eager expression. I started with the sound system, using words of action. They learned fast. Two mornings later the adults took down all the tepees, hitched the horses onto long posts, and laid the rolled up tepees across the posts.

The chief brought me some heavy leather moccasins and said, "This will save your shoes. The grass is sharp. My horses do not have steel shoes, so I put moccasins on my horses' hooves."

The chief announced, "Tomorrow, we go looking for buffalo."

BUFFALO HUNT

We heard a noise like thunder, and everyone stopped walking, all standing still like hunters. The chief dropped onto the ground and put his ears, first one, then the other, to the ground. He arose, saying in both Ojibway and English, "The buffalo are over there, coming in this direction to the stream. The herd is not very large. Be silent and get ready." All moved swiftly, uncovering a roll, and out came bone knives. The chief spoke in a whisper: "Those are our knives made out of bone,

13

very sharp. We make use of the whole buffalo carcass. We must make more knives."

The roaring sound came closer. We could hear the heavy hooves hitting the ground, then the heavy snorting of the buffalos' breathing.

The children had been ordered to stay down flat near the rolled up tepees, covering their heads with their arms. The horses were circled around the family with the hope that the leader of the buffalo herd would run around them.

The chief and his three oldest boys were standing up, ready with their bows and arrows to shoot at one buffalo.

The chief said, "We aim at the same buffalo only; if we used a gun the whole herd would spread out."

It was the largest herd of four-footed animals I had ever seen. Suddenly before us stomped a large buffalo. I never knew they came so big.

The chief was ready with his knife to make the animal bleed. A woman came running with several tin cups to save the blood, and each family member had to take a big swallow of the blood. The chief says it's good medicine. All the family members swarmed around the dead animal like vultures. Some peeled off the hide and flattened it out on the ground. The flesh was neatly sliced off the bones, and the bones were scraped clean and white and washed in the stream. The small bones were slit into small needlelike shapes. The hard hooves were used as sanders. The round knee bones would be used to grind the grain by rubbing on another bone. The rib bones were to be made into a papoose holder when the baby was carried on the back or it was used as a cradle. The hide was scraped clean of hairs when it was to be used for the waterproofing of the tepee or other rainproof articles. The hair was left on it if it was to be used for warmth. Even the entrails were cleaned, inside and out, to be used for clear ties or threads. The flat pieces of bone were sharpened on the edges and used to cut or to eat with.

14

At dusk everyone sat around the small grass fire eating the fresh roasted meat. The chief left the darkness and came back in an hour, handing the boys a drum he had made of the smooth, clean pieces of hide tied onto some short ribs. Then he showed them the low-sounding horn that he had made from the buffalo's horns. He handed his wife a small cup he had made of the other horn. For his daughter he had balloons made from the clean entrails, tied at both ends and filled with air. The long balloons were transparent; one could see the moon through them.

In the morning the smoked and dried meat was stored in dry leather bags.

I saw the Indians pick up the buffalo chips the herd had left at the watering hole and put them into burlap bags to use for fuel on the rest of the trip.

Chapter IV

Arrived at His Destination

Ben stumbled and shuffled into Edmonton without knowing or caring where he was. His shoe soles were worn off, his coat torn in strips, his hair long, his beard shaggy, and he knew he looked like a bum or even worse.

He led his exhausted animals to the stable. Without a word the stable man took care of the horses, and pointed out to Ben the bathhouse and the barbershop.

Ben forced himself to go to the store to buy new clothes. The shopkeeper asked where he came from. In a very tired voice Ben answered, "From Winnipeg, Manitoba."

The shopkeeper was stocky, with very dark hair. "You are too pale for an Indian, but you smell like one," he said.

Impatiently Ben replied, "I lived with some for some time."

Ben located the bathhouse to the rear of the barbershop. It was a rough boarded up shack with several round tubs made of wood. The barber filled a tub with warm water. Ben had to sit in the tub with his long legs. It was more like a sitz bath. The climax was having buckets of soapy water poured over him. A young man brought him a large mug of hot tea as he was relaxing in the warm water.

After the haircut and shave, Ben looked and felt like a new person. He found a boarding house where he could sleep and eat. Not until after a big meal of hot stew did he think to ask where he was.

He felt victorious when he learned he was in Edmonton, Alberta, and it was July 30, 1902. He figured out that he had traveled about 103 days but could hardly remember the last two weeks. It was real luxury for him to sleep on a bed with a mattress and have a big hot breakfast brought to his bed.

First his plan was to visit the land office and inquire for a job and about buying some land.

Everyone in this small town, which was called a township, was aware of the new young, blond, handsome fellow in town.

At the land office he was informed that he would not need to wait for a homestead until he was twenty-one years old, since he was almost twenty. He was offered a job in the land office but declined. He wanted to see how they farmed and procured horses in this prairie land.

He still had all his cash sewn in his heavy overcoat. He bought another riding horse and a packhorse.

The farms looked so meager, with small shacks or sod houses or just dugouts with flat roofs of sod. The shelters for the stock were small. He met up with several young men living alone in the sod homes. They were very friendly, anxious to see and talk to a new person. Not one of these young men complained about the hardships, but they eagerly talked about their plans for the future. Their dreams seemed very real to them. Their hopes for the future and the great freedom in the open spaces showed in their eyes and smiles.

Ben had several invitations to move in with them. They explained how difficult it was to turn the sod over to plant wheat or oats, which they had promised to grow in order to get their homesteads.

Every morning arising with the sun, Ben longed to see something green. It took the new grass a long time to show above the high last year's grass. There were no trees or bushes; everything seemed just to be a new beginning.

Edmonton had only one street, where a cloud of dust was stirred up when something moved. There were wooden elevated sidewalks by the retail buildings. The land office, barbershop, and bank each had space of nine feet by twelve feet with a rear opening.

There were a few families with children, but otherwise it seemed a male's world. There was a small schoolhouse with one window on each side, a sign of family life.

In front of each place were one or two sturdy posts to tie the horses to. In the backyard a cow or two were fenced in. The pigs and the chickens roamed around in the open. Ben wondered how they knew which pig or chicken belonged to which owner. There was some fencing in the rear of the buildings, mostly to keep the wild horses and cattle from racing through.

The man at the land office informed Ben about a new homestead area. He said, "Go south about a hundred miles or so to the township of Didsbury, where you will be guided to those sections of 160 acres you can choose. Here is a map, with crude but accurate directions to follow."

Ben was to start out following the Sunnyslope trail, an Indian path developed into a trail two wagons could travel abreast. Three Hills was marked toward the southeast of this trail as "a mining town." He was directed to go to the land office in Didsbury to pick up the list of sections available.

Ben knew that autumn was near, so he saddled up and was ready to leave in one day. "Winter starts here in September," he had been told several times.

Starting south, he felt the solitude once more. The beauty of the Rocky Mountains was a real pleasure, but brought out the cold emptiness of the distance. His riding horse was feeling the open freedom and wanted to speed up, but Ben kept him to a trot.

Ben could not forget the young farmers, who were called sodbusters, and their relentless struggle just to keep alive. None of them considered themselves to be living in poverty, but they all felt lucky to have the freedom to fend for themselves and considered this way of life complete. The violent cold was a challenge to adjust to, plus the calamities, but it all wove a person into a vigorous, witty, self-willed, and prudent soul. Each person had to be aggressive and ingenious to stay strong and alive.

Ben's spirits soared with the hawks appearing from nowhere and winging toward the snowcapped mountains. He had been told to follow the Knee Hill Creek, which would have a green bush here and there, and the flying population would always be drifting toward the water.

Ben was beginning to worry about the solitude and loneliness he had just gone through. "Will I be able to face this aloneness continuously?" he asked himself.

A few minutes later, he started to talk to himself again. "So here I am where I planned to come, with still no people, an uncivilized region without trees or waterways. Do I really want this?"

Suddenly he was jerked from feeling sorry for himself. Looking up at him without fear were six antelope, two large ones, two small ones, and two others in-between-sized. They started to dance and prance, leapt straight into the air, then darted away toward what Ben supposed was the creek. The antelopes' bodies were the color of the grass, but all had a white stripe on the head and the tail which could be seen for a long distance.

Ben forgot about his forthcoming primitive life, looking up in the sky and hearing the squalls of the Canada geese flying in a V-shape toward the water. He decided to turn in that

19

direction, too. The sun was hanging low behind the mountains, and Ben knew it was time to bed down near the creek.

Here again the prairie grass was very thick and high. In Edmonton they called it prairie wool.

He heard another sound in the distance like horses' hooves pounding the ground. There was a group of Indians, and they startled him. He had been told this was Cree territory.

At the Dominion Land Act (the land office) in Didsbury, Ben was directed to go to areas of Sunny Slope, Acme, Torrington, and Swalwell to look around and decide on which section he wanted. Then he should come back and the transaction would be made legal.

It took Ben a week to ride around. He met several homesteaders; some had settled well and made progress, but others had not fared so well.

Ben returned to the land office and was given section 33, township 30, range 25, and four steel posts with these numbers inscribed to be pounded into the ground on each corner of his 160 acres. He paid the fee of ten dollars and promised the government to break 25 to 30 acres of the ground to plant wheat or oats. He also promised to put up some type of building and to stay three years, not leaving for longer than six months a year. The papers were sealed, and now the place was all his own.

Ben was very excited and happy now that he owned his own land. He went to the lumber yard and bought enough to build a small house and barn, each to be twelve feet by fourteen feet, and promised the man at the lumber yard he'd be back to pick it up as soon as possible.

His nearest neighbors were five miles from his borders, others were ten miles away, but they all came to help build his barn and house. The neighbors volunteered to lend him a team and wagon to fetch his lumber. Ben, still in the stage of camping, had not much to offer, but the friends all brought food and extra fuel to cook it.

The beams, two-by-four planks, and the joists were put up on the first day. The boarding and the shingling were finished the second day.

Ben went to visit the Indian camp nearby; the Cree Indians had very good horses for sale. They welcomed him as a neighbor and showed him horses broken to work on the farm. Their favorite horses were the riding horses. The Indians collected wild horses, then broke and trained them for what was in demand by the white man.

Back at the homestead, the ten men working found time to tell stories and jokes and to tease each other. Two young bachelors got into a wrestling match. The men up on the ladders would cheer them on.

The older men found it easy to give Ben advice. He would not be bullied or run over by teasing. They found that Ben was very friendly but firm in his principles and opinions.

Ben learned from the experienced farmers that the grass in this area was nutritious and the cattle and horses would not need to be fed any grain.

It was a shock to Ben when he discovered that the creek on the map was no creek, just a dry streak, and the nearest water was one and a half miles away.

This brought out the story about a settler's starting to dig for a well with a shovel, digging twelve feet, and becoming too tired to finish that night. In the morning the well had collapsed. He climbed down to see what it was all about and discovered petrified whole trees. They took the wood to Didsbury to have it analyzed. It was petrified pear trees, years later put in a museum for posterity.

Ben took the large steel drum that the nails had come in, and with a few steel pipes that were left by an older man he built a stove.

The Indians had watched this project from a distance. Now they came closer, after all the others had gone. They had noticed that Ben had no glass for his cut out spaces for windows, and they brought animal skin so thinly shaven that it was almost transparent. They offered it to Ben for covering the windows, and he made the door out of leftover planks.

Chapter V

First Love

The October sun was rising in a tangerine haze, giving everything a touch of gold. The prairie was waving like sea waves. There was the quality of stillness that makes every animal and man pause to listen to the silence.

Many miles across this flat prairie, the majestic snowcapped Rocky Mountains seemed to wait forever, reflecting the golden beams like a beacon toward the images on the prairie. Ben was feeling like a king as he looked around him.

This year, 1906, the snow had not yet arrived, while other years snow arrived in September. The air was cold and sharp.

Ben was feeling the open space of freedom that all young men of the homestead craze always talked about, but he knew that this freedom meant cooperating with all the people around; each one needed the others. He also felt that this life of isolation and solitude had to change. He was spending too much time dreaming of companionship and would become depressed, as he saw no hope for his feelings to become reality.

As he came out of his twelve-by-fourteen house to do his morning chores, the silence everywhere made him put down the galvanized buckets without a sound and even stop whistling. With pride he gazed around his section of 160 acres, plus the extra 160 he had just bought. He had been here for three years, and the land was now his own.

The sunrise outlined everything in gold. The horses' backs sparkled as though emblazoned with gold. He loved the horses he had bought from his neighboring Indians.

He bowed his head and turned his face up into the cloudless sky and said, "Thank you, God, for all these blessings." In two years he had bought, bartered, and traded for two cows, two pigs, and a dozen chickens. He had one good crop of oats and lots of hay.

His cousin Abe had come here a year ago and found his 160 acres five miles away. Together they shared machinery. There were also their neighbors three and four miles away, and they all shared the farm machinery, too. Ben's hardest project was plowing the thick sod. He had a plow pulled by two workhorses. Ben's ambition and dream was to raise and train good horses.

There is always a quiet time to meditate while milking a cow, and suddenly Ben remembered there was a community gathering six miles away, where he would have a chance to talk and meet people. He enjoyed talking with the older pioneers and other bachelors.

He had a deep feeling of loneliness of late. This new mood frustrated him. He did not realize he had the God-given inclination toward and longing for female companionship.

As he rode the long pathway to his destination, his mind kept turning to thoughts of a young woman. The young settlers always complained of the lack of girls in this wilderness, but still their hopes kept rising to see one.

He could smell civilization before he arrived at the farm. Passing saddled horses and horses hitched to buggies, all tied to posts, he felt excitement at the prospect of meeting a lot of people.

The aroma of fresh roast beef roasting over an open barbecue made his stomach growl. In the rush of leaving, he had forgotten to eat breakfast.

There was food spread out on boards from one wagon to the next. The kitchen door was flung open, and a heavyset woman stepped onto the stoop and gave a loud whoop of a yell while holding up a steaming three-gallon coffepot. Suddenly a vehement gust of wind came around the house. Her long, heavy skirt, wrapping around her knees, knocked her off balance. The young men near her jumped up to help her. She was sprawled flat on the ground. The spilled coffee colored the ground bright brown. The woman was not hurt, but this did alert everyone that it was time to eat; whether her call was in Dutch, German, or English, it did attract attention.

An elderly man was slicing big chunks off the quarter of beef sizzling over hot coals. He looked like a hunter enjoying his catch, flinging a big butcher knife into the meat.

Ben was very hungry and was the first one receiving the steak with homemade bread and sauerkraut. He ate as if there was no bottom to his stomach.

Ben was so occupied attending to his appetite that he found himself sitting alone. Feeling like a stranger, he decided to remedy his aloneness by joining the others. First he stopped near the group of elderly men, hoping they would talk about their adventures in earlier frontier life. He introduced himself and they nodded their heads and continued to talk about this autumn's drought.

He next sauntered toward a group of young men, all about his age. They were lying outstretched on the grass. Their legs were still wrapped in leather riding chaps, and their spurs dug into the ground. Some were still eating and others laughing about the unseemly stories that only men would dare to repeat to each other. Ben did not break up the perfect circle of long legs.

He glanced away from the crowd; there before him was a young lady sitting erect in a sidesaddle on a tall, well-bred riding horse. She looked as if she intended to leave.

Ben thought she was an angel. Still towing his horse, he walked toward her. He saw the biggest brown eyes, which matched her brown hair and a complexion like a Dresden doll. She was dressed in a well-tailored gray riding suit.

Ben looked up at her with his winsome smile, introduced himself, and asked, "How about riding toward the west?"

Returning a courteous smile, she said, "My name is Helen Loen. I was born five miles from here. We live near the Knee Hill River." She challenged him to a race.

Ben was delighted to see her handle her horse as if she had been riding from childhood. He had never seen a woman ride an English sidesaddle. Her right knee hooked around the low handle, and the skirt covered her left thigh. He assumed she must be gripping the leather in order to keep her balance. She held her left foot relaxed on the stirrups away from the horse's body. Holding the horse's reins in her right hand, she kept her posture erect, as all good riders do. The horse had good lines and a fast walk, a springy trot, and a speedy canter. Her wide skirt covered the horse on one side, and the gray feather in her hat flew like a bird in the wind.

Slowing her horse to a walk beside Ben's horse, she said, "I have seven brothers and three sisters. I must be on my way home, as the sun is getting low." While she talked she observed the perfect profile of his very handsome face, his high cheek-bones, his thick, always smiling lips, and his smiling sky blue eyes. Taking off his broad-brimmed hat, he showed a head full of reddish blond hair. His complexion was burnt by sun and wind. He had strong, large hands and was tall, with a broad chest and a tapering waistline. His trousers fit snugly and his wool shirt needed laundering.

Ben asked in a slow, exact manner, "May I escort you home?"

Both knew it would be almost dark by the time they reached her home. Ben knew he would be asked to stay overnight, as that was the custom, with the farmers living so far apart. Ben had decided to marry this eighteen-year-old lady as

Helen Loen riding sidesaddle—1906

soon as possible. Staying overnight would give him the opportunity to meet the family and ask her father for her hand.

Reaching her home in the semi-daylight, he saw a big house on a hill surrounded by a white wood fence. The two large barns were a sign of a successful farm.

Two young men, looking more adolescent then teenage, were waiting by the gate. Sliding off her horse, Helen introduced her brothers. They quietly led the horses to the barn.

Her father met them at the door and shook Ben's hand. He guided Ben to the basin in a dark hallway to wash up.

Mr. Abe Loen (Helen's father) had a full auburn beard covering all the lower part of his face except a reddish nose and spots of rosy cheeks near his eyes. Ben felt that Mr. Abe Loen was a man of few words.

While Helen helped her mother with the dinner, Ben had the chance to talk with her father.

The dinner included Russian dishes, some Dutch dishes, and even a touch of German cooking.

Ben and Helen spent the rest of the evening getting to know each other, sitting by the riverbank under a bright October moon.

Ben touched her hand, trying not to show his anxiety, and blurted out nervously, "I know this is rather sudden to ask. Will you marry me? I already asked your father for your hand."

She looked up into his face, blushed, and shyly asked, "May I think about it overnight? I will give my answer in the morning."

His heart jumped a fast beat, for he was afraid to be refused and he realized she must have other suitors. But he felt that only she would fill that empty gap inside himself.

Ben shared the room with three teenage boys and had a restless night.

Helen knew that the decision had to be made now, as another young man was coming the next evening. Marriage was a lifetime commitment. Living with either man would not be an easy way of life. Her life with her parents had been a happy one, but she remembered the hardships of her childhood.

Breakfast was before sunup, and soon every person was out doing chores.

Ben thanked Helen's mother for her hospitality. He saw Helen brushing her horse and then taking off in a gallop. He hurried after her and greeted her with a whimsical smile as she slowed her horse to a walk. Her happy smile set him at ease as she said, "I will marry you as soon as you like."

He grabbed both horses by their bridles, swiftly pulled her off her horse, and embraced and kissed her over and over, taking her breath away. Then he stopped suddenly and straightened up. "Marry me in the month of March. That will give you time to make your outfit and give me time to fix up my house."

She swiftly jumped on her horse, turned it around toward home, and called out, "Come and see me often before that date!"

Helen did not tell her family about her first love affair, as it was not the custom in her family to talk about personal affairs. Her mother seemed very happy, always grinning and looking Helen over. Her father seemed pleased about her young man. The family took to Ben's free and friendly manners. Helen's father had invited Ben to come back and stay awhile.

In two weeks Ben asked his cousin who had a homestead near his section to look after his farm while he went to spend a week with Helen's family.

Ben moved about as if twitterpated, sprinting instead of walking and whistling gay tunes. The roosters and the hens cackled louder; the two hogs moved around faster, looking at the chickens as if they were silly; the cows mooed more softly. His horses neighed at Ben with nods.

Ben made plans to build an extension to his house; it would be the kitchen.

Chapter VI

Courting

The cold, dry November air gave Ben's horse the spirit to speed willingly to Helen's place in a short time.

Every morning during Ben's one-week visit the couple went horseback riding until mid-afternoon. They went along the river or crossed wherever it was shallow enough. More often they rode to the eastern prairie, where they could see as far as the eye could see, there being no trees, buildings, or posts to hold back the distance.

Once they stopped to have lunch where the grass was more than knee-high. The animals and the rains had not yet tramped down the dry autumn-colored grass.

They each broke pieces off a loaf of rye bread, took pieces of square cut ham with their right hands, held large cucumber pickles in their left hands, and alternated the bites. The pickles were called three-day Dutch dill pickles.

In between bites, they discussed their future life together and their dreams.

Every young woman knew her own future after marriage would mean keeping up the home and raising children, besides doing the farm chores. The young men dreamed of bigger farms with a lot of land and large barns.

After a sip of the homemade wine Helen's mother had put into Ben's back pocket, Helen challenged Ben to catch her while running. Her long, wide skirt looked like a loose umbrella. She could run faster but was teasing. He dragged her down, and the wrestling started. He was kissing her when a sudden crack in the air stopped all movement. The horses let out loud snorts.

They saw the grass had caught fire from the lightning crack and smoke in the distance was coming toward them. The bright flames created hot air. There was no crackling of flames, only a swish as the fire made its own breeze. As they galloped the horses westward, Ben instructed Helen not to let her horse see the fire, saying, "When horses see fire, they lose their sense and run into the fire instead of away."

Side by side the horses galloped. Pointing toward the east, Helen called out, "There, by the trees, is the river!" It was as if Ben's horse understood and surged forward, leaving Helen behind. Ben looked back and could see neither Helen nor her horse.

Turning back, he noticed the fire shifting southward instead of surrounding them.

He found Helen unconscious in the deep grass. He gave her some water and rubbed her neck and back until she opened her eyes. Then she sat up, looking as if she did not know what had happened. Ben said, "Stay there and I will check on your horse." The horse was on its side, grunting, snorting, and trying to get up. Ben touched the horse's back, rubbed it awhile, and talked softly until the horse's legs stopped kicking. He felt the legs up and down, finding a sprain on the front leg near the hoof. He took his bandanna, dunked it in the canteen of water, and wrapped it around the sprain, then urged the horse to get up.

Ben found a badger hole that the horse had stepped into, throwing Helen over its head.

The prairie fire was raging onward to the south, devouring everything in its path, cooking every prairie dog, badger, and rabbit that was not in its hole. In the deeper grass, the flames came as high as a person sitting on his horse. The lower flame had a yellow glow topped with a transparent blue.

Ben and Helen, leading their horses, arrived home very tired, with faces very red from the heat and clothing black from smoke, but after a clean-up they both felt better. After a substantial warm meal, everyone seemed to feel cozy enough to spend the evening sitting around the long kitchen table recalling early pioneer days. They all agreed that the old pioneering was like climbing the tallest mountain—one could not stop but had to keep going forward, and that forward had no end.

The day for Ben to return to his farm came, but he promised Helen he would return soon, before the wedding. Their farewell kisses were long and sweet, their embraces hard to unlock. Both felt their life together would last forever.

Back on his farm, Ben's enthusiasm for fixing everything the best he could in the limited time he had caused him to work night and day. He had a way of looking at the positive side of life and not having any negative views. He jumped over the snowdrifts to the barn as if he were the weight of a feather, whistling and running from one chore to the other. The deep snow kept the cows and horses from their drinking water, so Ben melted snow in his kitchen, carrying buckets of water to the stock.

Chapter VII

A Long Hard Winter

The months of November, December, January, and February of 1906-1907 saw very heavy snowstorms. Everything stopped and transportation was impossible. The battle to keep warm against constant winds was sometimes almost too much for human beings to survive.

The extreme, cold winters, summer hailstorms, droughts, grasshopper plagues, and early and late freezes were all taken as challenges to be fought in this savage country. The lack of transportation, of lumber to build houses, and of fuel for heat did not spoil their dreams. Money did not mean much because there was not much to buy. The silence in the wide open spaces brought the feeling of peace and freedom. Working out his own existence brought pride and self-esteem to a man. They were all poor in worldly goods but rich in expectations for the future.

Ben was looking out the window, leaning his elbows on the sill, thinking about the ground underneath the deep snow. The sky and the snow seemed to blend together without a horizon.

He thought of the hard work facing him in the spring, of plowing the twenty acres with a one-man, one-horse push plow. He had cut the grass for his horses and cows in September. After the heavy sod of this virgin ground was plowed, it would have to be chopped up with a pickax. Ben would need to borrow a cultivator to pulverize the big black clods.

He dreaded building a fence around the field to keep the wild horses and cattle from stampeding across, but just one stampede by them would turn it all to dust. He would have to dig many holes for the fence posts. He was convinced that this was the only way to have food for his stock and bread for his table.

He bowed his head, saying, "Thank you, God, for the strength in my body." Then he went back to scrub and polish the wide, rough boards on his floor, mumbling to himself, "I might as well fix and clean this place while there is nothing I can do outside."

He was getting solitude-happy, talking to himself again.

He raised his voice saying, "I will not need to talk to myself much longer. I love my Helen. It seems a long time to wait for the weather to let me out of here."

Ben mixed some soot out of the stovepipe with some leftover lard, making a good stove blackener. He tried to wash the windows, but the water froze stiff onto the panes.

He saw the darkness hide the earth's pale horizon. The northern lights shone with several colors, like a diffused rainbow. Nature offers everything in its way. Taking a positive attitude does help one enjoy nature's offerings.

The snow never leaves the tops of the Rocky Mountains. Ben felt that as it was now close to March, soon everything would lift itself to look up at the sun. His plan was to go to Didsbury, to get some lumber to add to the house and start a new barn as soon as the days got longer and the snow was cleared off the wagon trails.

Didsbury had the nearest railroad from whence came the mail—by sled, horseback, or later buggy. It took three days to deliver it and sometimes one week, depending on the weather.

In November, before all these snowstorms, word came that telephone wires would soon come near. The thought of verbal communication was like heaven when one was shut in by the long winters.

Ben opened his door and an old gray wolf stood in front of him, his eyes staring at Ben like strong beams. He quickly closed the door and went to find some food for the hungry wolf so he would not find his way into the barn for food.

The stars were very bright and seemed low and close. Ben knew that when the moon came up the wolves and coyotes would give out with their howls.

In the dim light of his kerosene lamp he started to plan for spring. His cousin would have finished building the new one-seat cutter Ben had hired him to make. The two new buggy horses would be mature enough to be trained to pull the buggy or a sled. His two cows would have their calves, and there would be plenty of milk in March.

On the first day of March, the Chinook wind arrived, clearing the snow very fast. The five-foot snowdrift between the house and barn was down to two feet, so it was easy to walk through it. Ben checked on his stock in the barn and found them all well. Now he believed that the hay was very nourishing, as he had been told. The animals had had only hay to eat all these months.

Ben saddled his horse and went to see his cousin Abe, five miles away. His horse had to watch its step. The ground under the snow made traveling like walking on a lake.

Seeing the wide, snow-covered fields, where no heavy sod plowman had turned or broken the soil to start the artifical crops, made Ben feel sad to spoil the naturally long-lived prairie grass and the prairie where the buffalo, Indians, and wild horses had roamed freely.

Chapter VIII

The Wedding

Ben arrived at Helen's on March 23 with his two newly trained horses, a brand new one-seated sleigh painted blue, and a big fur robe. He was wearing a dark blue serge suit and a celluloid collar in his shirt. He handed Helen a little package, saying, "I could not get you a ring, so this is something my mother left for me, and I have carried it in my pocket since I left home."

Helen opened the tiny package and sang out with a gleeful, surprised voice, "Just the things I needed for my new blouse!" There were six round pearl buttons with a tiny genuine diamond in the center of each. By the time dinner was ready Helen had sewn the buttons on her white silk blouse.

Dinner was a special occasion with the fresh roast of a veal calf which had been butchered two days before. The table was decorated with candles made of tallow and the best china plates that Helen's grandmother had brought from Russia.

On the twenty-fifth day of March at four o'clock in the morning, Helen and Ben were all packed and ready to travel, planning to reach Didsbury that evening. Ben had faith in his fast horses to make it home in one day. It was ten degrees below freezing, but heated rocks and plenty of comforters under the heavy bear fur robe made them confident of keeping warm. Lunches had been fixed and extra oats packed for the horses.

They arrived in Didsbury late that evening. The "hotel" was only a large home, but two rooms were available. Helen was feeling sick from being chilled, but a hot cup of tea revived her, and she slept rather late into the morning. After a hefty farmers' breakfast, there was a lot of laughter.

The bride's wedding suit was made of heavy wool jersey, well tailored by Helen, her older sister, and her mother. The jacket had a cinched in waistline, and the skirt had small pleats all around. Her white felt hat had a handmade pink silk rose, and her capelike coat was heavily lined to match the suit.

Together they walked to the office of the Justice of the Peace. There were several mud holes, and Ben picked Helen up and carried her over them. She was grateful that her high-buttoned shoes did not get wet.

At the door Ben bent over to kiss her, saying, "You are so beautiful, your dark eyes and hair stand out from your white suit."

She saw her reflection in the large front window and admired her small, stylish bustle and high heels, which were then in vogue.

It was a simple ceremony, performed by the Justice without a witness and with no wedding rings, on March 26, 1907. Proudly they carried out their wedding certificate without a word, only big smiles for each other.

They were expected at a small eating place next door for a very good meal and a small cake. The owner and the waiter greeted them with a song.

At bedtime Helen watched Ben undressing in the almost dark room. She was already under the covers. She was thinking with fierce pleasure of how handsome, tall, and muscular he was. She had never seen a man in the nude before. He pulled her close. She pretended to pull away, but her giggling gave away her willingness for the secret rite as old as time but always fresh and new between young lovers. These are the most precious moments human existence can offer.

Just married, leaving Didsbury—March 26, 1907

The newlyweds were awakened by a knock, as they had requested, at five in the morning, as this was the homecoming day.

The morning was beautiful and it was not freezing. They sang, whistled, laughed, and talked, breathing the silent crystal air, not minding the cold.

The snow was so hard it seemed as if the sled were skating, with a silent squeak and a swish. In the bright moonlight the horses acted frisky and willing to speed.

The coyotes joined in the festivities with high-pitched howls, and farther in the distance the wolves responded with lower howls, all toasting the happy occasion with their neighbors.

Ben had described his house to Helen in detail, but not too much, afraid she might be disappointed.

They talked in both languages, the Belgium Low Dutch and the English, depending on the expression they wanted to use. Helen did not know any of Ben's family members, so they had a lot to talk about.

The house and farm were all wrapped in darkness, and he had her wait by the door until he found a lamp. He then picked her up and carried her into a small but cozy kitchen. He showed her the bedroom with its brass bed. He told her, "Sit down and take it easy while I unhitch and tend the horses."

Helen was undressed and under the covers when he came in. He had a big grin for her and said, "This is very nice. Thank you for marrying me. I will not have to talk to myself anymore."

*　　*　　*

Helen opened her eyes and the sun was shining through the curtainless window. There were some movements by the kitchen stove and the smell of ham frying, and she saw her wedding suit hung over the chair. The air in the room was chilly, and quickly she put on a heavy robe. Combing her long hair, she followed the aroma of cooking.

Ben had finished all the outdoor morning chores and was in a relaxed mood. Both realized that now they were starting a new life together.

Chapter IX

Local Area

The hard winds and snowstorms came through the cracks of the house. Ben and Helen patched the cracks with rags and paper, pushing them in with a small knife. Ben put barn manure and straw around the house outdoors to keep the wind from blowing around and under the foundation.

The Chinook winds came often between the cold storms, which would cause the cattle and horses to sow their wild oats, running around with tails high and kicking their hind legs.

The young people had fun times even though they had to work long days on the farm. As long as the snow was not too deep, horseback riding was their favorite sport. The open fields lent themselves to easy racing. But there were certain rules that nature demanded, as they learned by bitter mistakes. When a half dozen riders would start racing, the wild horses in the distance, out of sight, hearing the thunderous vibrations from the ground, would be spurred to follow the race. The wild horses' running would bring out the wildness in the riders' horses.

One late afternoon, three young ladies and four men took a ride. For a distance they were calmly chatting, their horses walking sedately, so close to be almost touching.

The youngest girl, full of mischief and adventure, suddenly spurred her horse forward, which started all the horses to leap forward. She called out, "I will get ahead of you all!"

It did not take long for the wild horses to come out from the horizon. As the riders were facing the bright sunset, it was hard to see ahead, so they let the horses lead the way. Everyone was hanging onto the saddles with all their strength. Fifteen wild horses were following. Helen's horse was ahead of them all when suddenly he ran into a fence, throwing her over it.

Her long skirt got caught on the barbed wire, which tore it off up to her knees so her underskirts and ruffled pantaloons were showing.

The fence had been put around a new homestead without the neighbors knowing.

The other horses were leading the wild horses around the fence. When the horses had finally run themselves tired, the riders turned back to find Helen. She was not hurt, but her horse had a slight cut on his chest. Helen was very embarrassed, and angry at the young woman who had started all this trouble.

These settlers were all anxious to remove the sting of being called immigrants, so they spent long winter evenings studying to become citizens so they could take a part in improving the country. These people were from Sweden, Holland, Germany, Russia, and France and were all anxious to learn to speak English. The settlers from England let it be known they were already citizens of Canada.

The ones from Russia spoke Dutch and German. Their grandparents were called Mennonites. During the 1600s, the Empress Catherine invited them to come to Russia to grow the hard wheat the farmers specialized in cultivating. Hard wheat made the best bread. Soft wheat was used to feed the farm stock.

The Mennonites did not believe in carrying arms in military service. The Empress promised them exemption from all military service if they would bring the wheat seed and cultivate it in southern Russia. Groups of Mennonites and others came from the Netherlands, East Prussia, and Germany.

They lived and prospered in full freedom for eighty years while in Russia.

The Mennonites had traditionally migrated from one country to another to avoid persecution, secularization, and military service.

In the late 1700s the Czar discontinued the Mennonites' extra privileges and persecution began. Delegates were sent to Canada and America to check the soil in those countries. A Canadian agent was sent to promise them freedom from military service and the right to religious schools, subsidized traveling expenses, and twenty-six and one-third townships of free land west of Winnipeg in 1874.

Not all the Mennonites left Russia. They were not willing to leave their wealth and comforts. Those who stayed in Russia faced severe persecution and murder for many years after.

*   *   *

During the long winter evenings on the prairie, the women sewed quilts, knitted for the whole family, sewed all the family wardrobe, and even found time to crochet, tat, and embroider fancy items.

Laundering was a real hardship, what with carrying all the water in buckets and scrubbing each item with homemade soap. Ironing was done by heating heavyweight irons on top of the stove. The clothes were left out on the line to freeze dry.

The whole family learned how to knit their stockings.

The fathers and grandfathers spent the evenings fixing the leather harnesses. The young men constantly polished their saddles. Every young man had to have a horse.

The family history was always in the conversation. Many funny stories and sad stories were passed along from one generation to the next.

The preschool children learned to speak two languages mixed with English. Sometimes there would be two or three words of each language in one sentence.

*   *   *

In the spring of 1907 there was a late frost after a cold March and April. The summer brought a drought. The crop that had not frozen was a complete failure due to the drought. The garden did not produce. By September there was not enough to feed the stock. Ben had to sell his handsome buggy horses, and the pigs that had not matured were also sold. The older settlers who had more acres and had stocked haylofts would buy the stock from the young, beginning farmers. Ben kept the riding horse for transportation, and the two workhorses were a "must" for the farm. Their water had to be hauled from the river, five and ten miles away.

The mailing service from Didsbury was improved. It was delivered by horse and buggy, taking several days. The railroad that had been started from Manitoba in 1901 was now reaching Didsbury, and it was promised that it would get to Swalwell very soon. The telephone lines reached this settlement, bringing a real luxury to them all.

Autumn was near. Ben had to take a trip to get coal from Three Hills and lumber from Didsbury. In all it would take over a week to make the round-trip. He used his two workhorses and borrowed two more. He took the familiar and historic Sunny Slope trail. Another farmer also made the trip with his own team along with Ben. Ben and he had to sleep in the open some of the nights, but preferred to find a farm when they could.

Chapter X

A Trip for Coal

One night Ben and his friend settled down in a farmer's barn and slept in the hayloft. Ben could not sleep because his partner snored too loudly. Ben shook his friend, Mr. Brown, awake, and he jerked and sat up, saying, "What's the matter, you can't sleep either?"

The mystic calmness in this early autumn morning before sunrise made Ben feel the solitude. If he made a sound, it would crash and echo for a long distance.

Both men saw the long straight line of raised earth, and they waved toward it with a happy smile, understanding that it was the beginning of the railroad track going toward their homes.

Stopping by a creek to water the team. Ben saw a peculiar mound of white pieces. On closer study he saw it was a side of bleached bone. He could see a complete skeleton and skull of a buffalo, one bone on top of another. He had heard of buffalo hunters slaughtering a buffalo, just taking the tongue, as a delicacy to eat, and sometimes the hide. He knew now why his Indian friends despised the buffalo hunters and fur traders. This was indeed unnecessary destruction.

This was an ideal place to set up camp, near the small creek. Without speaking, each man started to back up the wagons and make a V-shape with the unharnessed horses. Each had four horses. They laid out the heavy bear rugs on the ground.

A soft breeze came over the one-inch-deep snow. A small fire of grass sticks heated water. Coffee made from toasted grain and dunking dried bread made a good meal.

The moon was unusually bright, which brought out the night music from the coyote and the wolves. Both men were sleeping heavily when they suddenly heard the horses being restless.

Ben called, "Mr. Brown, what do you want?"

Mr. Brown glanced over at Ben's bed and answered in a soft voice, "I want nothing, but do not move. You have a big bear standing on top of you."

After a few minutes the bear moved off and trotted away with a low growl. Ben's tiredness had left him. He went for a stroll and saw two large wolves sniffing around the pile of bones. Ben pulled out the small deer rifle he carried. The wolves ignored him, stopping to drink and then leaping across the creek. Ben realized that all animals had plenty of food this time of year, with young rabbits and rodents coming out of their homes in the ground.

Ben and Mr. Brown started off at sunup to get to Three Hills by evening.

They saw the wagonloads of coal being pulled by mules coming from the mines and being emptied in three separate hills. One hill had very big chunks, another had medium-sized chunks, and the third had fine stuff almost like dust.

The town of Three Hills was only a small settlement with a few houses. They found room in an old clapboard building that had two extra bedrooms, but no stable for the horses. They were tethered to the wagons and fed hay and oats.

After good food and a long rest, the horses and men were willing to move and load the wagons. Going back, with a heavy load, would be much slower. By the time the sun was setting, they had gone only five miles. Seeing a narrow road like a lane to a farm, Ben turned in until they saw a small shack with the

A bear on top of sleeping Ben

chimney smoking. There was a lot of movement of horseback riders. Getting closer, Ben saw they were Indians, his friends. They seemed glad to see Ben, explaining they had been trying to talk to the woman inside but could not understand her language. Ben knocked at the door and called out in Dutch and then German.

Suddenly she opened the door, looking very scared and in tears, but happy to see a white man speaking her language. She said, "I just recently came from Sweden and cannot talk English. My husband left for a few days, and these Indians frightened me."

Ben calmed her, explaining, "These Indians are harmless and my friends. They are asking you if you are interested in buying some horses."

She answered, "No, my husband went someplace to buy a workhorse."

Ben visited awhile with the Indians, and then they left.

The woman introduced herself as Maria. She had arrived a month ago and married her husband. She was so grateful to see Ben and Mr. Brown that she invited them in to stay for the night and cooked some potatoes and a slab of bacon while her guests unhitched the horses. It was a one-room house with two windows and one door. She went to bed in the corner with a curtain hung on a rope around her bed. The men brought in their sleeping blankets and slept on the floor near the stove.

The next was another sunny day, but autumn was in the air. September was usually when winter started, and one could smell winter coming. They had to rest the horses frequently, for the road was rough, with deep wagon ruts where the wheels got into the ruts and the horses could not pull the load off the ruts. Mr. Brown would unhitch his four horses and hitch them in front of Ben's team to pull out the stuck wagon. After Ben's wagon was free, then all eight horses would pull Mr. Brown's wagon out of the muddy rut.

The third day a red-coated mounted policeman met them, saying in a rather angry voice, "You are under arrest for working on Sunday."

Ben looked very puzzled and asked, "For *what*?"

"Don't you know it's against the law to work on Sunday in this township?"

Mr. Brown came to Ben's wagon and explained, "We have come a long way and are trying to get back home as fast as we can go. We did not realize that this was Sunday, and we have never heard of this law in the whole province. We have families that we must go to."

The policeman blushed and apologized. He mentioned, "We have a strong new group of people that recently moved into this area; they are strict with the rules of life, and I have been ordered to try to keep the peace. They are another new cult. Their dress code is more important to them than religion. They are all living in a commune and wearing black clothes with no buttons, no frills. I cannot tell which man belongs to which family, as they dress exactly alike, so that one cannot tell one from another. It's a very queer set up; they call themselves Hutterites. They demand strict rules." The policeman, looking very handsome in his bright clothes, saluted and rode off, saying, "Have a good day."

* * *

Helen stayed home alone until her water supply ran out. Ben had brought water in a wagon from the creek a mile away. She had used some of that water to water her garden, as it was drying out from lack of rain. She had used her time to clean the house and do some extra laundry. Then, being without water, she went to her brother's ranch, miles away. She was approaching the house when she saw a woman's silhouette coming down the slanting road. The woman was swinging a butcher knife, howling, yelling, and chasing after a coyote, screaming at the animal, "Don't you dare kill my sheep!" The coyote could not take that furious onslaught and escaped, leaving the sheep intact.

After sunset, Ben's team, with a slow crawl, arrived home. There was no light and no wife to greet him. Getting his team into the barn, he was too weary to worry about anything else.

In the morning he was awakened by the bark of his collie, named Sport. Helen marched in and started breakfast with the last bucket of water. Ben and Helen were very glad to see each other. It seemed to both that the separation had been very long.

The drought continued. The usual October snows had not arrived yet. Prairie fires were frequent. Those farmers who had cut their hay earlier hoped they would have enough to feed the horses and cattle. The gardens yielded only a small crop of potatoes and turnips. They butchered the calves and pigs rather than sell for a low price. Ben announced to Helen, "I will have to sell all the cows and horses and leftover hogs. The creeks are dry; there's not even water to do the laundry."

Helen was feeling very sick. In November she told Ben, "I am going to have a baby, and I am three months on the way."

Helen could not keep any of her food down and lost strength every day. By December she would not bother to raise her head or try to talk.

Ben had his hands full trying to keep the small number of stock in the barn alive and give Helen the courage to eat. All she had eaten in a week was some barley broth.

On December 15, the air seemed to have changed. He looked out the window and saw nothing but a curtain of snow. He ran to the door and had a hard time getting it open, even though it opened inward. The snow had come so fast that all he could see was a six-foot-tall drift before him. He jumped with glee, whistled, and cheered until Helen called and said, "What is the matter with you? Why are you acting so silly?"

"We have snow, lots of it, and water for us and the stock."

Ben did not try to dig a tunnel but climbed over the drifts. He was wise enough to take along a shovel to dig a snowdrift away from the barn door.

The cow had given birth to its calf, and now there would be milk. He caught the old rooster, convinced that it would make some chicken broth for Helen. He still had five hens left to lay eggs. The eggs he found were frozen solid, but he picked them up anyhow.

The snow kept coming for several days. Every farmer and animal hibernated as best they could or froze to death. There was no way to have a community Christmas. New Year's passed without Ben and Helen seeing another soul.

By the second week of January, the snowdrifts had been blown away by the cold winds.

Ben knew that he should try to contact the midwife, the only one in this area for many miles. He looked at the calendar to see that the baby was expected in three or four months.

He was still worried about Helen's condition, asking himself over and over, "What if the baby arrives too early? What would I do?"

He had this constant depressing feeling that this year, 1908, would be an unusual one. Sitting on a stiff kitchen chair, elbows on his knees, clasping his head in his hands, he contemplated the future. He had always been chipper and frank, without prejudice and ready with his friendly smiles, but he was losing it all. He kept repeating to himself, "I am at my wits' end; I do not know what to do."

Chapter XI

A Son Is Born Too Soon

The first day of February, Helen started moaning and then screaming with pain. Ben took a deep breath, held it long enough to calm down, and started to make plans.

Helen called and said, "I know the baby is coming; get the torn sheets in the bottom drawer."

Ben argued, "It is not yet time. Take it easy, take a deep breath, and convince yourself that it's only a false alarm. I have no way to get the midwife, because the roads are still all blocked."

All day and night Ben cooled Helen's head, stroked her arms and legs, and gave her some headache pills. Finally he figured that he had seen and worked with the cows when they were giving birth to their calves and that it couldn't be too much different.

Early on the third day, he was prepared with the sheets and towels Helen demanded. Helen gave a strong push and then sighed with relief. Ben saw the tiny baby and wrapped the baby in a warm, soft woolen blanket. He saw Helen was lying so very still, hardly breathing, but asleep. He cut the cord. The baby seemed to be breathing, but its skin looked blue and transparent. Ben could not tell if it would live. It was only two hand-lengths long. He sat next to his wife's bed watching them both.

He really did not know how big a newborn baby should be. Everything seemed so calm and quiet, and he was so exhausted he fell asleep, leaning his head on Helen's bedside.

He was jerked awake by Helen shaking him. She smiled and said, "I am hungry. Give me my baby." Ben was afraid to give her the baby, expecting it to be dead. When she held the baby in her arms, he went to cook her some ground wheat cereal and hot tea. She said, "The baby's chest is moving up and down, and its hands are warm." Holding her baby in her left arm, she ate her food with gusto.

"The baby is so very small." She asked for the kitchen scale. Together they wrapped the baby in a diaper, tied a knot, and hung it on the scale. Happily Helen said in a soft voice, "Here's your four-pound baby boy." For the first time in several days Ben smiled.

Helen tried to nurse the baby, but he was always asleep, so she took his head and puckered his lips to wake him. After the second day, he started to suck her breast. Ben was delighted to see his son hold his finger and then saw that the baby's nails were transparent. They named their son Bernard.

The baby had not made any sound of crying. Ben kept round stones warming in the oven, wrapping them with towels and setting them around the little body to keep it warm.

Each day there were more signs of color on the baby's skin. Ben would give the baby a few drops of warm water sweetened lightly with syrup from a dropper.

Every night Ben awoke from a nightmare that his baby had stopped breathing.

One morning the baby moved his arms after leaving his mother's breast. Ben gave a whistle of joy, telling Helen about it, and for the first time in months she showed a smile.

Climbing over the snowdrifts to feed his stock in the barn, melting snow for water to do the laundry and for his animals, and feeding his wife and baby, Ben started to think about food.

Rocking her four-pound baby boy

Food was the most essential thing in this world. *Adam and Eve in the Bible had only food on their minds. God first invented food, then man. He made animals for man's food and food to grow for the animals. There would be no world without the growing food. Food, food everywhere, and even then, nothing would grow without water. There would be no life without water. Without food there would be no present or future. Human beings, just like the animals and birds, work hard for food,* he mused.

Looking down at his four-pound little one, Ben said to him, "Even you stay alive from the little nourishment you can take." He was still not sure if his first born would live, and felt the chances were slim.

* * *

The first of March was a crystal clear morning. The melting snow from the roofs had left icicles hanging around everywhere. When Ben stepped outside it was so silent that if a sound were made, it would come crashing down like tingling icicles. He took a deep breath, and the cold air filled his lungs with a pleasant pain. He felt that all the vast space stretched out to him, making the struggles of life worthwhile.

The snow sinking into the ground brought back all the hopes of a good crop for the farmers. Ben planned to restock all the stock he had sold.

On the twenty-sixth of March, a dozen farmers came to see Ben and Helen, bringing them food and gifts to celebrate their wedding anniversary. Everyone was surprised to find the new addition. Ben explained that the little boy was almost two months old and had not been expected until April. "He is still so weak that he does not cry, only gives little squeals like a rabbit," Ben said.

The farmers had gathered here to discuss crops, share the machinery, and trade and breed horses, cows, and pigs. The women talked about saving eggs for new chicks and planning their gardens.

Life was simple. There were no garbage cans or garbage collections; there were no bottles or tin cans to dispose of, nor piles of newspapers. If there was any soft paper from magazines or newsprint it was cherished for wrapping eggs to save them for spring hatching. For toilet paper in the outhouses the Eaton catalog was saved, and it also served for a wish book while one was sitting in the outhouse.

The leftover food from the table was given to the dog or dumped into the slop barrel with vegetable peelings and grains for the hogs. Even the dishwater was mixed into the slop barrel.

There were never old clothes left to be thrown away. The worn out coats, pants, and sweaters from the adult clothing would be remodeled for the young ones. The good parts of clothing were cut into small pieces with designs to make beautiful quilts and covers for the feather or wool comforters.

The mattresses were of heavy ticking sewn together as a sack the size of a bed and stuffed with straw. The shoes would be repaired or the good parts saved to patch the leather harnesses or saddles. All the hand-knitted stockings, long ones for children and women and knee-length for men, would be darned over and over until there was more darned wool than sock. The neatly patched and darned clothes were a sign of a good, economical wife; ragged, unpatched clothing was frowned upon.

To dry-clean a suit of wool or a felt hat, a mixture of salt and kerosene was brushed on the soiled spots, then brushed off.

The leather came from slaughtered cows, horses, and pigs. Some made beautiful soft leathers. The furs came from wolves, foxes, rabbits, and badgers. Fur luxuries were the bear furs and buffalo pelts that fur traders and Indians brought around to sell or barter.

The ladies found it a great pleasure to save flour, sugar, and salt sacks and lay them on the grass or snow and let the sun bleach them. Beautiful embroidery with crocheted edges was made into aprons, underwear, dish towels, luncheon mats, and children's clothing.

Furniture was made by anyone who volunteered to be the carpenter. The wealthier immigrants had brought good furniture from Russia and Germany.

There was no government welfare or insurance. The settlers either could not afford it or did not believe in it; nor did they believe in suing anyone. A man's word was his honor.

By this time the citizens were anxiously awaiting the railroad tracks.

Kerosene and salt were as precious as gold, and it was usually a community endeavor to transport them from the nearest town or settlement. Kerosene was for the night-light and as a disinfectant.

Chapter XII

Lea Arrives—September 21, 1909

In September of 1909, the morning light crept through the lace-covered window in the small three-room cottage. Ben struggled out of bed, trying not to disturb his young wife. His year-and-a-half-old son was asleep in the far corner on a small homemade cot.

Ben was trying to shave with his long-bladed shaving knife in his right hand while stocking the coals with his left hand. The iron kitchen stove was slow getting hot. He grinned into the small mirror on the wall while combing his blond hair. His beard had a stubble of light hair that hardly showed, so he had to feel where he needed to shave.

The sun was rising in the tangerine haze—a sign that autumn was here. He looked toward the eastern pasture to his new horses acquired from his Indian friends.

After feeding all the stock and himself a hearty breakfast, he noticed Helen looking pale and tired. "Do me a favor and phone for the midwife. After all, we did get the phone for this purpose," he said. He knew the baby was due any day and hoped for a better beginning for his second child than his son had.

* * *

He was dragging a spool of barbed wire and a borrowed fence post digger. It was a hard job digging holes in the deep sod. Ben looked up as he was stretching the wire tight. He saw Helen coming across the deep grass. She stumbled and fell. He dropped everything and ran toward her. He saw that the baby was coming and knew now what to do. He cut the cord. Taking off his jacket and covering his wife, he instructed her, "Stay still until I come back." Taking his sweater and wrapping the baby, he hurried to the house. Looking down at the baby, he saw a healthy chubby little girl with eyes wide open as if she were enjoying the fresh air. The cradle was fixed with soft pink blankets. The baby gave a strong cry.

As he ran back to Helen, he saw his son playing in the dirt, using a spoon for a shovel, unaware of what was going on. The new mother seemed all right, with an almost smile as he carried her into the house.

Ben named the baby Lea, which meant "open space" and "open meadow." He wanted it pronounced the Dutch or the Swedish way, "lay-a," not the English sound, "lee." She was the first white girl born in this Indian territory.

Lea grew fast and very normally, and her vigor was a joy to her parents. She was chubby and always smiling, with rosy cheeks. She ate everything within her reach. She had a pink complexion, blue eyes, and reddish blond hair. The only time she would cry, or rather scream, was if she was denied something she wanted. She would then roll and kick on the floor, but her mother never gave her any heed until she was too tired to move. Otherwise she never seemed to find a reason to cry.

One time the door was open. She crawled outside and up a pile of ashes near the house, then stood straight up. Laughing and feeling victorious, running down that mound which seemed a mountain to her, she never crawled on all fours again.

With her keen curiosity, getting into every cupboard and drawer and watching her mother's activities in the kitchen, Lea

59

seemingly learned to observe without asking questions. Fascinated, she watched her mother constantly pour pots of food and liquids into a big barrel on the porch. To satisfy her curiosity, she pushed a chair next to it. As she was looking down into it, she lost her balance. Helen heard a gurgling sound and saw two little feet sticking out of the barrel, so she pulled Lea out by her feet. After a lot of spitting and coughing, Lea controlled her breathing.

Forever after Grandma teased her with, "The reason Lea has such rosy cheeks is because she fell into the barrel of pig slop."

Lea was two years old when her sister arrived. The sister, like her brother, was skinny and of pale complexion and not healthy and rosy like Lea. The two were always sickly and never ate well. The brother's name was Bernard, and the sister's was Rachel. Their father sent all their birth reports to Edmonton, the capital of Alberta. He also recorded each birth in the back of the family Bible, which was the traditional way of keeping family records.

Lea watched her baby sister with wonder and pinched her to see her reaction, but could not understand why her dolls made no response to her pinches.

Lea was playing with beads on twine. Helen taught her to string the beads, which was boring to her. Being an adventuresome little soul, she put one blue bead in one nostril and a red one in the other, discovering that these caused a shrill whistle. She ran to her mother, laughing, and pointed to the beads in her nose and said, "Listen, Mother, to my whistle."

Helen grabbed the child, held her very tight, and with tweezers slowly pulled out the beads. She gave Lea a good smack on her buttocks and scolded, "Never do that again."

Lea often played quietly with her dolls and doll buggy for several hours at a time. One nice sunny day she found three small kittens squirming and squeaking. Gently, with her soft

The kittens that Lea unintentionally drowned

little hands, she stroked their backs, murmuring a very soft lullaby. She put her dolls on the ground, dressed the kittens with the dolls' clothes, laid them in the buggy, and said, "Now go to sleep. I will drive you around." But the kittens would not lie still. Seeing a bucket full of rainwater near the rain barrel, she got the idea of giving the kittens a bath. Being bathed one at a time, the kittens wiggled at first, as if the ice cold water was too much for them. After the kittens stopped struggling, she dried them with a doll blanket and covered them up in the doll buggy. Lea marched very proudly toward her mother, saying, "See, my kittens are sleeping now."

Chapter XIII

A Tragic Event

The proud young father and good husband suddenly became ill. He complained of a severe pain in his right side. After being in agonizing pain all night, he had Helen phone the doctor who lived ten miles away. She explained the pain, which alarmed the doctor. He said, "I will get there as fast as possible." He hitched his fastest horse to the lightest buggy, and even at that it seemed a long drive. There was no moon and no northern lights, but the stars were very bright.

The doctor examined his patient and ordered Helen to scrub the kitchen table and bring out all her clean linens. "We operate immediately; his appendix is ready to burst," he said. In his black bag the size of a suitcase he carried all his operating needs. After an hour's operation, Ben was carried to bed. The doctor left with orders that Ben stay in bed for a week.

Before the week was past, Ben could hear his horses in the barn, restless and kicking against the barn walls. He could not wait anymore and insisted on getting up to check on his horses. Helen objected, "You are not strong enough to walk." He could not walk straight but walked like an old man, all bent forward.

He walked between the horses, speaking with a soft but commanding voice. He passed a young horse next to the wall. The young untrained horse pressed close to the wall, squeezing Ben until he was crushed. He was too weak to push the horse

The family watching Cornelious Ben die—1912

aside, and he screamed for help. Helen pushed the horse away and dragged Ben into the house. Then she telephoned the doctor.

The doctor made arrangements to have Ben taken to a hospital in Winnipeg, Manitoba. His ribs were crushed and piercing his lungs.

Lea stood beside her father, talking softly. She could not understand why he did not get out of bed. Somehow she knew that he needed comforting and stroked his face with her small hands, saying, "Daddy, please get up soon."

Grandpa and Grandma arrived to drive the family to the nearest railroad station, in Swalwell, from where they would take the train to Winnipeg. A bed was fixed up on the floor of the wagon. Ben was in constant pain during the rough ride, and the train ride meant more the same. By the time they arrived at the hospital, a high fever had set in. An infection had started in his pierced lungs. He went through several operations.

While Helen spent all her time in the hospital to be near her husband, Benny (as Bernard was called), Lea, and Rachel stayed with Ben's uncle and his family. Lea would be a good girl all day long, playing quietly with her brother and sister. At bedtime, though, she would start screaming, "I want my daddy! I want my mama!" She would continue to scream until exhaustion put her to sleep.

The doctors at the hospital claimed that they could not do anything more to help Ben. A tube was inserted below his lungs so that the infection could drain out. The family was shipped back to their prairie home, and after many months of illness, he knew he would not live long. Helen spent a lot of time silently gazing upon her dying man's face. She sensed that he was battling for his life.

One day a so-called minister, leader of a fanatic religious cult, came to call. The minister, first of all, told Ben to convert and that he would go to hell if he did not get rid of all the evil things he possessed—things like jewelry and photographs. The minister ordered Helen to wrap up in paper all her jewelry and family photos and bring them to him, as they were of the devil. Then he made a large bonfire outdoors while making a lot of loud talk with his face and hands pointing toward the sky. He grabbed all of Helen's things and threw them into the fire. She was so brokenhearted that she wept for several days. All the things she had wanted her children to have in memory of their dying father were gone.

Lea and Rachel played quietly, close to Ben's bed, as if they could feel the sad surroundings. Sometimes Lea stood by her father and they would look at each other for a long time. Helen heard her husband tell his daughter in a very weak voice, "You will bring many people a lot of sunshine." He lifted his head slightly, seeing little Rachel crawling toward him, pulling herself up on the bed sheets, and he smiled. His son sat in a corner with his small head between his knees, as if weeping, while his thin body shook with grief. Ben took his last breath with a deep, audible sigh.

The burial was held in the open prairie cemetery. Grandpa, Helen's father, was holding Lea in his arms. No one else could hold her, as she was constantly wiggling and wanting to run around. Lea was watching very closely when the men started to lower the coffin into the ground with ropes. Other men began to throw dirt onto the coffin. Suddenly, with one leap, screaming, "I want to go with my daddy," she landed on top of the coffin. Several men jumped in after her and handed her back to her grandfather. This scene caused the group surrounding the grave to let out a terrible sad and loud moaning and weeping. Before this they had been silent. The women were all dressed in dark or black heavy coats with heavy woolen kerchiefs which almost covered their solemn faces. The men, lips tightly pressed together, did their obligatory duties in burying the young man. Everyone loved this departed man, as he had been a good leader of the community. Everyone was aware that the young widow with three young children would have a harder time to face than ever before.

Four-year-old Benny was motionless, neither crying nor speaking, and had to be carried away. He did not speak a word for many weeks after the burial. When he started to talk again he had a stutter, which remained with him for the rest of his life.

Helen had cried herself out in the nine months of her husband's illness, knowing for many months that he was dying. She had no more tears to weep. After the funeral, her parents helped her and the children into the backseat of the buggy. Without speaking a word, Helen held her children close to her body.

Helen's parents did not go into her house, as they had to return to their farm before dark. Silently the widow walked into her house, squared her shoulders, and determined to face life alone with her children.

Benjamin Piner had been a board member for the district school. He had high principles. He fired a teacher who spent too many hours being too drunk to teach well.

Ben was tall, with broad shoulders and narrow hips like a Swede. He had heavy lips and a big smile showing a friendly, determined, and sincere mouth. He was outspoken and had a very hearty laugh. If challenged to a fight, he never faltered or hesitated to face any danger. His captivating smile and blue eyes seemed piercing when he looked anyone square in the eye.

After the nine months of being so very ill in bed, his body shrank to the size of a child and his wife could pick him up and carry him like one.

Quoting Helen's brother from a letter:

Ben would never let a bully run him over, and if it came to a showdown, he took a lot of punishment without complaint. He suffered a long time with his abscessed lungs, and there was no medicine in those days to help him.

His last words to me were, "I hope to see you in heaven."

I drove the wagon to the cemetery carrying him in a homemade coffin that my father made.

Ben Piner died on July 27, 1912.

Chapter XIV

A New Life

Helen did not go to bed this night, but sat by the round kitchen table. The light from the small kerosene lamp made her face look ghostly white. She had before her all the record books, which Ben had kept in order—all the assets and expenses. By sunrise she had recorded all the hospital and doctors' expenses which had to be met, including the debt she owed the hired men who had done the farm chores while she took care of her husband and children. She knew she would have to sell most of the stock and maybe some land to pay for the hospital and doctors' bills. The funeral had not been any extra expense. Her father had built the casket, and the small lot for the grave was free.

She looked around in a daze with her pencil still in her hand. The lamp on the table was burning its last drop of kerosene. Blowing out the smelly lamp, she went to the door and saw daylight starting. She took a deep breath of the fresh summer air.

The house was very silent, and the door into the room where her dear beloved had breathed so heavily for nine months was closed. He had been too weak to talk the last few weeks. She asked herself, "Will I ever forget his long-suffering and heavy breathing?" Many times when she could not hear him breathe laboriously she would run to him and touch him to see if he had died. Covering her face with both hands, she let the tears roll and, without control, she moaned and silently screamed.

Opening the door again, she heard the cows moo and the rooster crow, all telling her that they and her children needed her. She put on her barn coat and shoes and picked up the milk buckets.

She recalled while working that it was July 27 when he died, only three days ago, and it seemed like an eternity. Through the night she planned her budget and figured how she would settle up her debts. She counted the pigs, cows, and horses to see how many she would need to keep, and she would sell the extra 160-acre section. These plans and the outdoor work helped her forget her pain.

Leaving her work clothes at the door, she smelled the hot Postum and steaming cereal. As she bent over to fill her cup, she heard a twitter and a happy squeal. All three children were under the table laughing at her. They were partly dressed and the two oldest had helped little sister down the steps. Helen could not hold back a smile.

She was determined to give her children a good life. She knew it would be hard. There was the daily chore of pumping the water for the stock and household use. Although she had had hired men to do the barn work before, that would now be her chore. Her lot was to push the wheelbarrow full of manure out of the barn, carry the buckets of food to the pigs and chickens, and be the farmer, hired man, housekeeper, and mother.

Watching her three children eating the rolled oats with gusto, she squared her shoulders and felt stronger. She now realized she must make do on her own ingenuity.

On laundry day many pails of water had to be pumped from the well to fill the oblong copper kettle which took up more than half the space on the stove top. The hot water was dipped into the round galvanized tub filled with dirty clothes, and she rubbed each piece on a washboard.

Twice a year she made a large batch of her own soap. The white soap made of pure animal tallow was used for baths. The yellow soap was made from pork lard mixed with lye and was used strictly for laundering. Helen made the soap only while the children were not around. It was too dangerous with all the lye. She would mix these ingredients in a large round iron kettle outdoors and boil it, constantly stirring, for several hours.

The Indians often came racing across the prairie as if chasing something, starting at sunrise and heading toward the sunset. They homesteaded their land in the Indian fashion, but they loved to go west toward the river, ten miles away, to fish. In the wintertime a few Eskimo wandered down from the north, but they preferred not to stay long.

The summer brought gypsies who traveled in white covered canvas wagons. They had four horses pulling and many horses tethered in the rear, with small foals following the mares. A large family lived in a single covered wagon. The gypsies made their living by selling horses to the farmers. Stories would spread that the gypsies stole chickens and all the food they could eat. Ben Piner had always preferred to trade with the Indians rather than the gypsies.

One early morning Helen heard a commotion near the barn. When she came out, she surprised some Indians who asked for her husband. The Indians spoke the English language well. She told them that her husband had died and she could not buy any more horses and offered to sell horses back to them. One of the Indians' packhorses was carrying a moose carcass. Two of the Indians removed some of the hide from the moose and cut a big chunk off and set it down by the door. Sympathizing with the lonely widow, they promised to be back in a few days to buy her horses.

Helen did not own any beef cattle, only enough cows for the family milk and butter, so she was grateful to get some fresh and different meat; otherwise the daily meat supply was pork and chicken. She put the hunk of meat into her oven, completely filling it, and baked it for a week. It was still too tough to cut up. Jokingly she would say, "The only way to tenderize moose meat is to let the dog drag it around for a week, stomp on it for several days, chop it with an ax for hours, have a strong man grind it in a meat grinder, and then cook it for two weeks."

The children learned to entertain themselves by inventing their own amusements. The few toys and dolls they had were bought through the Eaton catalog from Winnipeg, Manitoba. There was a lot of time; no outside world events and no community, church, or school affairs interfered. Visitors were seldom and far between. Their mother spent as much time as she could afford teaching them and reading the Bible and the Mother Goose books and other children's books to them.

Benny, at age five, had a brainstorm of sailing down the creek. Dragging the large, round galvanized laundry tub into the water, he sat in it and sent it drifting to have his joy of sailing. His constant companion was Sport, who was a good watchdog. After he had sailed a distance, Sport got alarmed and started to bark, running back and forth from the house to the creek until he got Helen's curiosity aroused and she followed the dog. When she saw Benny sailing wobbly in the distance, she started to run along the creek edge until she caught up. She jumped into the water and dragged the boy and the tub ashore but did not scold the child, understanding his desire to sail.

Helen was advised by everyone to move the house and the barns to an area west of their section of land where several other farms were situated. Her friends and relatives felt that she was too far away and too much alone at the present place. Helen's relatives arrived to move the house. With large spikes they lifted the small three-room house onto several long logs and rolled it down the slight but long decline.

She had sold all the horses except two buggy horses and one riding horse. She kept enough cows, pigs, and chickens for food for the family. After the house was rolled five miles to its destination, it was left sitting on the logs until the next day. The following morning the men came back to set the house on some large rocks used as the foundation. Both the logs and the rocks had to be transported from a long distance, as there were no woods or rocks nearby. Lea was sitting on a high chair in the kitchen as the house was lifted and dropped. The motion of the house frightened her. She was found having fainted on the floor. The rest of the day she was kept in her mother's bed.

For two weeks Helen had to drive her buggy back and forth to where the animals still lived. By the third week, the barn and all the animals were settled on the new farm area. The neighbors across the road helped her to feel at home. The children adjusted to the new place and loved to run in the neighbor's garden with big trees planted in rows all around it.

At four years old, Lea had to use a small knife to dig out the dust and dirt from the cracks between the wide kitchen floorboards while Helen scrubbed them with a big brush. Eventually she had linoleum put on the kitchen floor. The children had a lot of pleasure sliding on the new, shiny floor, especially after Helen washed it. Often she would leave the bucket of scrub water standing at one end of the floor. The children took this opportunity to play ring-around-the-rosy, encircling the bucket until they would fall over from dizziness and knock the bucket over. More fun ensued on the wet floor, which always ended up with all three being punished.

Morning and evening Helen would bring in two pails of fresh milk and pour it into the large, round aluminum tank sitting on top of the separator in the far corner of the kitchen. The children loved to turn the handle around and around, which made the cream come out of one spout and skimmed milk out of another. Lea would run to fetch her cup; she relished the warm skimmed milk, although Helen always saved whole milk for the children to drink.

Cream was mostly saved to make butter, the churning being another chore for the children. After several days, enough cream was accumulated in a two-foot-deep stone crock to make butter. This stone crock had a lid of heavy wood with a round hole in the center for a stick to fit in. The stick was pushed up and down in the cream until the butter gathered and separated from the buttermilk. Lea was still too short to reach the stick, so she had to stand on a chair. They had a round wood mold into which she patted the butter until it was even and smooth. The mold had a flower imprint to give the top of the butter a sculptured look.

Relieving oneself meant going to the outhouse in all kinds of weather. The outhouse was built of rough boards and stood across the yard from the house. One would tramp through deep snow at forty to fifty degrees below zero and sit down on a high box type bench with a round hole in the center. Through the wide cracks of the boards, crystal snow blew in and hit one's bare bottom. The toilet paper was the stiff pages of Eaton's old catalog. In the summertime it was smellier, but one could look through the Eaton catalog as a wish book.

It was natural for the small children to hold back their nature's call, which prompted Helen to give her children laxatives often. Lea was very stubborn about taking pills, so Helen would grind the pills and put them in Lea's sandwiches. When Lea tasted the bitterness it caused her to be afraid to eat sandwiches.

The heating stove was downstairs, and the only warmth the upstairs got was through the black stovepipes leading into the chimney, which was enough for the daytime. For the night the coal stove was banked so that the coal wouldn't burn up through the night; therefore no heat reached upstairs.

Helen kept bricks in the oven all day; at bedtime she wrapped them with towels and placed one at the foot of each bed. Everyone learned to wrap themselves with two-inch-thick woolen comforters, making them like tents so they could turn over without disturbing the cover. In the morning on rising they could see their breath floating through the room. It was taken for granted that everyone kept long woolen underwear on, even under the flannel nightgowns. The woolen undies served as a second skin, and many people kept them on all winter without even a bath or a change. Helen, however, being conscious of cleanliness, changed her children's clothes every week after the weekly bath.

The weekly baths were taken in a galvanized round tub placed near the kitchen stove. The hot water was dipped out of the tank built into the stove. Lea caused problems when her mother started scrubbing her tummy. She would start to giggle, and the more her mother scrubbed her, the more she giggled, until she became hysterical and ended up getting spanked.

Lea's bed was close to the window and of the same height so that she could see the scene down below. Most every morning in the wintertime a fox would be sleeping by the window just below her. As soon as the dog arose and came around the house, the long chase would start across the open snowy field and Lea would wake the family by cheering for the dog, though she did not want the dog to catch up with her friend the fox. If in the night a wolf would howl, Sport became a coward and ran, with his tail between his legs, into the barn.

In the winter the snowcapped Rocky Mountains, far away across the wide open fields, would look very blue, with snow-caps as white as the clouds. In the summer the forest fires in the foothills would cause a gray haze, dimming the white-covered mountains.

An elderly man, Benjamin's uncle, came to see the family from Winnipeg. Lea sat on his lap and played with his eyebrows that hung over his eyes. She called him Big Uncle, as he was a very large man. He gave Lea two new copper pennies, each the size of an American quarter. She delighted in shining them up by rolling each one in her mouth and then rubbing it dry with a handkerchief. Suddenly she called out, "Mama, Mama, my penny got lost in my mouth!" Helen immediately checked and sure enough, there was only one penny. Lea repeated again, "It's gone through my mouth," pointing down her throat. Helen held Lea upside down, shook her, and rubbed her chest and throat without any result. She phoned the doctor and he said, "There is nothing we can do but wait to see if she will expel it through her bowels, so keep watching her bowel movements." Her mother agonized with worry for three days, and finally the penny came through just as shiny as could be.

When the snow was too deep and too soft the children could not play outside, so they learned to entertain themselves. At four years old, Lea mastered the needle and scissors, sewing clothing for her dolls. She also spent many hours sculpting animals and people out of plasticine. When she was six her aunt taught her to crochet and Helen taught her to knit. Benny spent his hours whittling in wood. He carved dolls out of softwood for Lea and Rachel. The little girls cut paper dolls out of the catalog.

Helen made all the clothes for herself and the children, ordering the materials from the catalog and knitting all the stockings, mittens, caps, and sweaters. But the shoes had to be ordered, as the children grew out of them fast, which often resulted in their wearing too small shoes. The shoes came ankle-high for dress, in leather with buttons on the side. For the cold weather the shoes were of felt, edged in leather at the sides and with leather soles. If they happened to have them, they wore rubber shoes over the felt, which made the warmest

Lea and Benny creating

footwear. Otherwise, the felt shoes too easily absorbed moisture, causing the feet to become chilled. Helen had not learned as yet to insulate with layers of down feathers or sheep's wool in their coats of tweed.

One day Lea went along to town with her mother. The town, Swalwell, was only ten miles away, but it took one and a half or two hours to get there by horse and buggy. Lea's eyes opened wide to see so many houses on each side of the road. After tying the horse to a post near a store, Helen took Lea's hand, saying, "I am going into this store. You be a good girl and stay close by." Lea had no idea what a store was nor that it had things like candies and fruits to be sold. She was more interested in the clopping noises that footsteps made on the wooden sidewalks built a foot off the muddy ground. She ran ahead, jumping and hopping on the sidewalks, echoing and magnifying the sound of each step. Lea spent all her time running up and down the sidewalk until her mother came out of the store with her arms full of packages. Lea laughed and giggled at each stomp. She never again saw a town or a store until her teenage days.

Early spring brought out the new piglets, roaming and squealing in the yard, and the baby chicks in their small wire pens. The calves were constantly making themselves heard.

The long daylight hours of the northern summer days, which lasted only for July and August, were filled with activities. Instead of forming figures in clay or mud, in the summer, Lea would form things in her sandbox with wet sand.

Lea's favorite toy was a doll as big as herself stuffed with fine cut rags and called a rag doll. Her mother had embroidered the face, and the hair was of yellow wool in two braids. It was dressed in Rachel's outgrown dress. One evening Lea left this doll in the sandbox, which was very unusual, as the doll was always near her. In the morning she found her doll mauled to hundreds of pieces by the pigs. After this, whenever she had to throw garden-fresh turnips to the pigs she scolded each pig with a nasty word.

Helen built a frame like box with chicken wire on all sides and the top to allow the little chicks to get sun and air. Often Lea would find a small hole large enough to put her hand through to reach and touch the fluffy little yellow things. The mother hen would come running from her sheltered box, and other hens followed, scolding and flapping their wings, shedding a cloud of feathers all around. Lea spotted a small chick outside its pen, and as she picked it up to put it back in the cage, several mother hens suddenly flew at her, knocked her down, and started pecking her arms and legs. She screamed. By the time Helen came around, Lea was on her back; a dozen mother hens were on top of her, pecking, scolding, and flapping their wings on her body. Needless to say, Lea never went near the small chicks again.

Each child had certain chores to do as soon as they could handle obstacles and animals. Brother Benny was to bring all the cows into the barn from the pasture fields in time for the milking, which meant getting up with the sunrise and working until sundown. His dog, Sport, did most of the chasing to get the cows home. The horses automatically knew that was the time to come near the corral for food and water.

One of Lea's chores was to pick the eggs out from under the setting hens in their nests; they often objected to this thievery and pecked her hands. She had been warned about a fox or a coyote being in the chicken barn. The door was always kept closed, but if the animals were small enough they could sneak through the hole cut out of the wall for the chickens to go in and out. If there was such an animal in the coop, the instructions to Lea were not to scare the fox or coyote, which usually crouched and trembled in a far corner as soon as it heard someone approaching. She was to back out of the door very slowly and call for help.

The most worrisome creatures were the weasels, who could slyly crawl under the hens and suck the eggs. Lea was warned to first examine the hen before putting her hands under to reach for the eggs, as weasel bites were painful and dangerous. Helen set up steel traps for the weasels. For the coyote or fox she preferred to open the door to let it out, but she had a good gun with her in case of an attempted attack by the animal. She was very jealous about food for her family and would protect the supply of hard-earned food.

The chickens, eggs, and milk were the most important of all the food; second came the grains, wheat, and oats for bread and cereals; thirdly the meats, pork and beef. Fruit was seldom to be seen. Apples would be in the cellar as long as they lasted. Dried fruit would be bought at stores in large bulk. The vegetable most easily grown and kept for the winter was cabbage, which often ended up in sauerkraut and had the best of vitamin C to be found. Sugar and sweets were seen only on very special occasions.

The summer days were long, so Lea and Benny found time to invent their own ideas. While knocking off the potato bugs into tin cans with a small stick, working close together, they would plan and scheme very secretly. One of their ambitions was to build a high teeter-totter; another was to try to swing until it turned over the cross log.

They found a heavy ten-foot-long board and put a box, usually an apple crate, under the board and kept adding more boxes until the board was as high as the chicken barn. While Benny held down one end of the board Lea would climb up to the end of the board and let Benny know when she could see the roof of the barn. If it was not high enough, she would slide down and help him put another box on top of the other boxes. When Lea finally could see over the roof, a very delighted squeal and laughter were heard. Helen's attention to what was going on was attracted by the victorious cheers.

Their swing was made of heavy round poles ten feet high with the same size pole crossing on top from one pole to another. In the center of this cross pole a heavy rope was wrapped around it. The swing came in a double length so that a four-foot-long board was attached and several people could sit on it. Lea and Benny would stand on each end of the board and keep pushing to gain more height with each push. Their aim was to go so high that it would turn over the crosswise pole. That was the ultimate of high swinging, despite Helen's orders not to do it as it was too dangerous. When starting the high swing they knew their mother could not stop them except for scolding with her fists. Lea's looking at the big sky up so high gave her the feeling of being a bird.

The light in the house after dark was a small kerosene lamp with a long, narrow glass chimney which was to give more light from the flame. It was Lea's responsibility to keep that thin chimney glass shining clean, as her small hands were able to get into the chimney. She broke many of them until she learned to put less pressure on the glass. The daylight lasted until almost midnight, and everyone was up with the first light from the sun.

Now communication was by telephone; each family shared a party line, with as many as six families on one line. This was how the news and gossip was spread, as everyone picked up the phone when it rang and listened in. Helen taught her children to answer the phone after two short rings and one long. Everyone knew the other families' rings. One would be one long and two short rings, another would be three short rings, and so on. The gossip and news spread, often into unrealistic stories. The telephone was hung on the wall, and the children would have to stand on a chair to reach the receiver on the side and speak into the speaker that was sticking out in front.

The children had no awareness of world affairs until they started to attend school when they became seven or eight years of age. Visitors were very few and mostly in the summer months. The children always played outdoors in good weather, so they seldom heard adult conversation. The only violence they were aware of was weather and wild animals.

The dog had all his freedom to roam around, sleeping in the barn when weather was bad, but sleeping next to the door of the house in pleasant weather. The dozen or more cats also lived in the barn and were fed the milk during milking time. The job for the cats was to keep the mice away. The mice would multiply too much in the wheat bins and often came into the house through the basement. It was the responsibility of the oldest cat to keep the mice out of the house. No one worried about keeping the cats and dogs warm enough; their warmest home was in the barn with the cows and horses.

The horses also had their jobs. Two horses would pull the sled in the winter. They were heavy horses but not as heavy as workhorses. Another horse, taller and lighter in weight, pulled the one-horse buggy. The tallest and most slender horse was for riding and for going to the pasture to round up the cows. Helen leased out the wheat fields to different farmers, so she did not have to worry about workhorses.

This was before the Industrial Revolution, and the simplicity of life bred a simplicity of needs, so temptations were limited. The children's daytime dreams, their imaginations, built in the open skies, were their very own, free to roam as far as the mind could invent without suggestions or instructions from other minds or the outside world. Their minds matured and thinking progressed according to natural physical growth. The children were not pressed to face fears or concerns beyond their understanding and so remained happy much longer than children of today do.

The first gusty winds in August told the farmers to harvest the wheat and cut the grass for hay. The cattlemen (called cowboys) could be heard in the distance with their whistling and calls to drive the cattle to the market.

As soon as the farmers cut the grass and raked up the hay into rows, Benny and Lea would find binder twine, a rough, fuzzy string, and make a round noose at one end to use as a snare. It was easy to find the prairie dog holes in the ground after the hay was raked together. Benny would take the initiative in putting the noose over the hole to show Lea how it was done, and then he laid down on his stomach at the other end of the string about five to ten feet away. As soon as the prairie dog popped his head out of the hole, Benny would give a quick yank on the string, which lassoed the prairie dog's head. Most of the time the prairie dog gave a sharp whistling shriek before his head showed, which seemed to call out the neighboring prairie dogs. The children had at least two strings to pull. If the noose had not broken the prairie dog's neck, then the dog would be lying low nearby to take the rodent and swing it back and forth until it was dead.

The prairie dogs could ruin a wheat crop if they multiplied too fast. So the game warden would pay the children a penny for each prairie dog tail they brought in, with a stern warning to make sure the prairie dog was dead before pulling his tail off. The field snakes would be nearby to swallow the dead prairie dogs. Frequently the children would sit still in a corner of a section and count the prairie dog heads popping out of the ground. They were the size of rats with long, furry tan hair and bushy tails. There was no poisoning done to depopulate these rodents. It was up to the dogs and the children to do their best to control the prairie dog population.

At harvesttime, the large steam-engine tractors pulling the threshing machine coming toward the farm could be heard for several miles away, causing great excitement for the children. Helen had been cooking and baking for the threshing crew for days, and the aroma of the baking gave everyone a great appetite.

The tractor was the size of a railroad locomotive, with a large black stovepipe standing up high, where the smoke puffed out clouds of black circles. A man steered it into the fields between the rows of wheat sheaves. Another man shoveled coal into the belly of the tractor. Several men would feed the sheaves, which had been cut, tied in bundles, and set in rows the day before, into the threshing machines behind the tractor. The tractor and the threshing machine were connected by a foot-wide belt around big wheels; the power came from the tractor motor. One large funnel would spew out the wheat kernels into a deep wagon. When the wagon was filled, two horses pulled it to a wheat shed that had a dry bin for storage, while a second wagon quickly pulled up beside the machine under the funnel. The larger funnel was pointing high into the air. It had a blower blowing out straw until it formed a stack as high as any house.

Lea and Benny had to carry a big, burdensome bucket of lemonade and a basket of cookies across the stubbled field where the crew was busy at work. Five-year-old Lea spilled a lot of lemonade, as she had to use her knees against the galvanized bucket to help push it forward. The workingmen, upon seeing the refreshments coming, stopped the engines and enjoyed the rest. Benny and Lea hungrily watched the men devour the cookies and lemonade. Sometimes someone would take notice of the hungry look in the children's eyes and invite them to sit down and enjoy the feast.

At the noon hour when Helen had the dinner all on the table, Benny would run toward the crew and wave both arms to signal that dinner was ready. The small kitchen was filled from one end to the other with a long table set up with boards on sawhorses, seating all twelve men. The children had to wait to eat until all the crew left, with the hope that there would be something left for them.

The following morning was the time for a thrilling experience that the children anxiously awaited. It was to get up on top of the new, loose straw stack, then jump down into it by climbing the roof of the barn. The straw was so soft and fluffy that a child would sink way into the stack. Helen worried about this, as a child could suffocate before finding his way out. So Lea and Ben planned it so that if one jumped then the other would watch below to check the spot where he landed and count to ten, and if the sibling did not show, then the one below started to dig him out. This was their most exuberant thrill of the year, and they always managed to find their way out of the stack.

The day after Christmas, December 26, Helen hitched the horses to the large sled that was boxed in all around. She made warm beds with heavy blankets. The comforters were made of Helen's father's sheep's wool, and the pillows were filled with goose feathers from her mother's geese. Helen had warmed several stones in the oven the day before and placed them between the blankets in the sled; all was ready to go to her parents' for a family reunion.

It seemed a long, long ride for the small children. They would constantly pop their heads out of the covers and ask, "Almost there, Mama?" She would push their heads back under and yell, "Shut up!" as she was too busy holding the reins and guiding the horses on a solid snow road, watching out to go around the snowdrifts and then get back to the path that was the main road.

As a tradition long in the family, each grandchild had to memorize a long poem, called in German "Weihnachts Wunsche," meaning "Christmas Wish." Lea had been trying for a week to memorize a wish that had ten four-line verses. It being in the German language, she couldn't understand what she was saying except the few words her mother had explained. It was hard for Lea to remember it all. She recited it over and over and worried about it until her head ached. If a child did not recite it perfectly, standing in front of Grandfather at attention with hands folded in back, he would not get his bag of goodies until it was said without a mistake. Lea was more bothered with the thought of all her uncles, aunts, and cousins sitting along the edges of the room on stiff chairs, laughing at the mistake. These recitations seemed a dreaded nightmare to the smaller children.

Lea looked forward to one thing, and that was that Grandma always had Lea sit close beside her. It was fun to talk with Grandma, as she understood one's feelings.

When they arrived in front of their grandparents' house, several uncles came out and carried the children in, still wrapped in their blankets, and unhitched the horses.

The gathering was in the large kitchen, which had two stoves, one a cooking stove and other a heating stove. The table was long enough to seat thirty people. Grandpa was sitting in his rocking chair in the parlor, the very special large room that was used only for special occasions. He had a very long red beard covering most of his face, and only his red nose stood out.

Grandma came and wrapped Lea and Rachel in her large apron and led them to the stove. She held them close while rubbing their hands until they were warm enough to hold a cup of warm cocoa.

Lea's lips remained down at the corners of the her mouth. She was still worried about her long recitation, wishing it were over with. Then Grandpa called the clan into the large parlor. He was sitting almost in the center of the room while other chairs were lined up close together along all four walls, leaving the center of the shiny varnished hardwood floor for the grandchildren to line up. Grandpa seemed in a good, jolly mood and did not bother correcting the children's recitations as they stumbled and stuttered with the difficult language which was so strange for them to understand. So Lea relaxed and recited her verses, smiling all the time and looking straight into Grandpa's eyes.

The Christmas dinner was a baked goose stuffed with whole apples, mashed turnips, and parsnips. The children were served mashed potatoes instead of turnips. Also there was sauerkraut, carrots, and other canned and pickled vegetables. The children were trained not to talk when adults were talking. The children also had to wait for their food until all adults were served, but Grandma seated the children at the table end near the stove so that she could serve them the tidbits they liked best.

Before the sun had set behind the trees on the hill across the river, all the clan had gone home except Helen and the children, who stayed for the night. A bed was made for Lea in the upstairs hall. It was a cold place and Grandma kept putting another blanket over Lea every time she passed her bed. Lea finally went to sleep between the noises of the grandfather's clock down the hall. She had a nightmare and woke screaming; she had dreamed the blankets had got so high that they were touching the ceiling and choking her.

Chapter XV

Lea Stays with Grandma

Lea loved to stay at Grandma's. Ever since she was four years old, Lea was taken to Grandma's whenever Benny or Rachel was sick. When epidemics like mumps, measles, scarlet fever, chickenpox, or smallpox came around, Benny and Rachel would be very sick for a long time, but Lea would seldom have a fever and would be over with the disease in three days. So she spent the time until her brother and sister recovered at Grandma's.

Grandma ate very slowly at mealtime because of poor-fitting teeth. Lea always sat very close to her grandma and thus learned to eat slowly, too. After everyone had left the table, Grandma and Lea would go into the basement with the excuse of picking the rotten apples out of the barrels. The basement had no cement walls; its sides and floor were plain dirt. Wooden shelves reaching as high as the ceiling were filled with jars of fruit and pickles. Barrels of cucumber pickles stood about. Grandma would slip away behind a curtain where she was making her own wine. After a little time she would come out with a jar and a cup and sit down on a wood apple box to slowly drink her precious nectar, pointing to Lea to continue to hunt out the bad apples in the barrels. This was a secret ritual every evening.

In the morning, the three uncles and Grandpa came in for breakfast after having done the chores of milking the cows. The meal was usually fried chitterlings, fried potatoes, and applesauce with heavy, dark bread.

Lea was very curious and observant of the surroundings and was filled with a desire to quietly go exploring. Her experiments often got her into trouble. This morning she tiptoed out to the summer kitchen where Grandma did her cooking and canning in the warm summer. She found a door and walked through a dark, cold corridor where heavy work clothes, saddles, and harnesses hung on the crude walls. She came to a very heavy-looking door, pushed on it, and fell into a cold, dark hole. It was packed with straw and big square chunks of ice, with round hams and other parts of meats and butter. The cold made her gasp and cough, and then she screamed. A sudden light caused her to blink, and there stood Grandma with a lantern, reaching out her arms to pull Lea up.

One day Lea saw the men disappear through a deep passage of snow dug open like a tunnel. She followed the passage, with sides so high to her that it seemed like there were mountains on each side. She felt very small and alone but kept running until she slipped and landed on her seat and smack into a double door. She pushed this way and that way until the door swung open wide. There she saw rows of cow behinds wagging their tails as if in unison to music. Cautiously she touched a bent hind leg and suddenly felt herself being thrown several feet into soft cow dung.

She walked around to the front of the cows. Their heads seemed bigger than herself. They stared straight into her eyes. Each cow's head was clamped tight by the neck so that it could only look ahead between two boards. So Lea felt safe enough to walk to the other end of the barn. She stopped to watch each cow chew and chew and then take another mouthful of dry hay from the manger and chew some more. Continuously the brown plops kept coming out of their behinds. She asked herself, "How can the milk that comes out of the big pink bags under the cow taste so good and look so white?" But the smell of the barn answered the question why Grandma made the men take off their clothes before entering her kitchen. Looking straight into the eyes of each cow, she said, "Your eyes do not say anything," then continued walking.

Looking up, there was a square hole and a built-in ladder on the wall leading up to it. The boards seemed rather far apart for Lea's legs, but by climbing she reached the top. She could only see big squares of hay and straw piled high on the sides. In the center the long floor space had smooth and shiny boards, and she discovered it was good for sliding to the other end. Sliding, she went straight into another square hole in the floor, landing in another crib of hay in front of a group of horses, startling them and causing a lot of noise. Grandpa came in to check on the horses and found Lea in the crib, covered with hay. Lea took off up to the house as fast as she could run.

When Lea was at Grandma's in April, the ice would start to break in the river. Large slabs of ice would break and roll down the river. Several foot-thick pieces would move along and bang against others, causing a thunderous noise. This could go on for days and weeks. At times one slab would rub another, making a high-pitched screech. The river sounded as if it were angry. Those nights were sleepless nights.

Grandpa and the uncles had to make sure they had cut enough ice squares for the icehouse out of the frozen solid river before it started to break apart. Often a coyote or a dog would be seen floating on a broken off ice slab, looking frightened, cold, and wet. It would find a way to jump from one slab to another until it found one near the bank. Sometimes the animal missed the goal, fell between two ice slabs, and was crushed instantly.

With the signs of spring Lea would emit a great bubbling up of enthusiasm for everything she saw in nature. The hills and prairies lost the dull colors and showed new emerald green grass everywhere. Lea would look for the wild blue crocuses peeping their heads out through patches of snow. She would dance from one crocus to the next until she had her hands full of the soft blue flowers.

Another spring treat was to see the small new green chives showing out of the ground. Lea would butter a slice of whole wheat bread and go out to pick one stem at a time and lay it on top of her bread until it was covered with these onion tips. After not having anything green all winter, one's system craved some greens.

One beautiful, clear, sunny morning, Grandma was washing and ironing Lea's new dress, which had an all-white Alice in Wonderland style apron that wrapped around and over her dress. Grandma ordered Lea to stay clean, as guests were expected to arrive. Lea was very anxious to get out in the sun to play, so she wandered outside. Playing ball and skipping rope soon bored her. She noticed a big gray bird flying toward the river bend and decided to follow it. She started down the hill where Grandpa was pounding and clanging with a steel hammer over a red-hot fire. He explained to her that he was making iron shoes for the horses, but shoved her away because of the sparks. She hurried down the path where a horse was going around and around, hitched to a long post. In the center were two big, round stones that were grinding grain. The grain was dribbling out from between the stones. Even though she had not spoken, her curiosity showed on her face, so her uncle explained what they were doing. At the same time he noticed Lea keeping her eye on the bird above. She was advised not to go in that direction, as the eagle lived there and "he will steal you and carry you away." Lea only laughed and ran on. Reaching the river, she saw a tree with a big nest. She climbed up the tree and put her hands into the nest. Making a round basket out of her white apron, she put all the eggs in it, climbed down, and ran home to show her grandma the new treasure. When she

Lea showing Grandma the crushed bird eggs in her clean apron

opened up her apron to show her, all the eggs were crushed and the yellow-stained apron brought a very cross look from Grandma, who yanked off the apron and ordered Lea to go upstairs and stay there for the rest of the day.

Lea loved to be in the garden while Grandmother worked in the flower beds. There were small paths around each circle of flowers, and Lea loved to run, hop, and sniff each flower. Grandma loved flowers and had every window loaded with potted plants. She often said, "If they do not have flowers in heaven, I don't want to go there." As Lea ran around them, she would pick some, then hide underneath a bush. She would spend hours making little slits in the stem of each flower, then delicately putting the next stem into the slit until she had a long enough string of flowers to put around Grandma's neck.

Lea was used to hearing Grandma scold and nag Grandpa about something or other, but Grandpa never got the chance to talk back and went off mumbling into his red beard. His red nose was always ahead of the beard. Lea never sat on Grandpa's lap, as his long beard frightened her.

It was Grandma who told her the stories of long ago when she was young. That there had been times when she was five years old and there was nothing else to eat for a long time but fish out of the river.

After a warm rain, the fun was to run and splash around the water puddles barefoot. Lea ended up playing in the mud. The adults called it "making mud pies," but she denied making pies, claiming she made animals and people.

One day, sitting on the bank of the river, she noticed red mud. She started playing with it and discovered that it was much smoother to the touch and smelled cleaner than the black mud. Lea made large forms, finding that it kept its firmness. She wanted to share her exciting find with Grandma, but was told to go and wash the red stuff in a basin of water.

Lea would watch them skate from the upstairs hall window. A phonograph and food were taken along. A big bonfire was started by the bank of the river. It lit up the area like a crimson lake. The men shoveled the snow off the ice. The young people skated till late, and Lea went to sleep leaning her head against the windowpane.

That thing they called a phonograph had Lea puzzled. After the men had gone out to work the next morning, she tiptoed into her uncles' room, which was forbidden territory. She stopped in front of a square box with a large, shiny horn and a wide opening at the top. On the side of the horn was a picture of a white dog listening in front of a horn. Aunt Anita, Helen's younger sister, startled Lea as she was concentrating on the queer machine. Asking, "Would you like to hear this thing?" Aunt Anita put a flat black disc on top of the box. It went around and around when she wound the crank. Then a singing voice came out of the horn. Lea jumped aside and backed off, then stood still to listen. She liked the music and started to giggle.

*   *   *

The reflections of the bright sunlight on the snow caused one to squint the eyes at the vast area of just snow. The three uncles, Aunt Anita, and Lea headed back toward the east on the roadless sea of snow to Helen's house. The uncles spoke excitedly about the party that night.

Helen had put a big beef roast in the oven, so big that it filled it up entirely. The aroma of the cooking brought on a high spirit of celebration in those coming in from the cold drive. Most of the men arrived on horseback, wearing jingling spurs made from Mexican silver and leather chaps made from rough leather with the fur on the inside, fitting over their pants in front and tied around the legs to keep the cold wind from penetrating to their legs while riding horseback. Helen had strict rules that the men leave the spurs and chaps by the door. The spurs would cut holes in her linoleum floor, and the chaps had too strong a smell, as they were never washed. The men who came with girlfriends or wives arrived in sleighs.

All types of games were played for entertainment at the party. The children were allowed to watch these games until bedtime. One funny game was the wet sock competition. A knee-length knit sock was stuffed with wet rags. While blindfolded and on their knees, two men would try to hit one another. Whoever gave up had to give the wet sock to the next volunteer until everyone had been challenged.

In the midst of this happy party there was a very heavy knock at the door, then more by the window, as if the house would come down. Cousin Peter Piner opened the door. Three heavy, tall, very angry Indians threw a body into the door, screaming, "Is this one of your men? He is a very mean horse thief." The body of a man about forty years old was so badly beaten and bloody that none could recognize him. The whole party assured the Indians he was a stranger, and then the Indians disappeared.

At first the body seemed lifeless; then someone spoke up, saying that he saw the man's eyelids move. The women hurried with pans of water and rags to clean up the bloody, muddy form. The women then found his pulse still beating.

Since most of the party stayed overnight, sleeping on the floor and packing the house like a box of sardines, the motionless form was set in the farthest corner.

After three days the figure showed signs of wanting to talk. He turned out to be a wandering person of the kind who were called bums. No matter what his hard luck stories were, a horse thief could not be forgiven. That was an unforgivable sin, and his name would be on the blacklist.

In a week he left as he had arrived. He did not leave a name but was referred to as "the horse thief."

*   *   *

The young homesteaders did not feel destitute or denied luxury, even if they did not have a luxurious way of life. They were proud of their accomplishments in tilling the new land of roadless spaces. They had the freedom to act on their own ideas and no government or territorial laws to hamper their initiative. This gave them self-esteem and an earthy humor.

Not one of them had ever experienced wealth or city luxury and so had no regret or temptation, but only looked ahead into the new future. All took pride in their small hand-made houses. Many were made of squares of earth mixed with sod, and others were built of clapboards. All the men would always talk about how and when to enlarge the house and the barns or secure more land and farm stock.

The relentless struggle to adjust to the hardships and the many calamities in the wild surroundings, the unsteady climate of the long winters and snowstorms, the strong winds in spring and autumn and early frosts fostered ingenuity and the aggressiveness to work harder.

The population of three young men to one young girl gave the females plenty of suitors. For young wives it was a lonely way of life, for sometimes they would not see another soul for months.

The apprehension of illness in the family, accidents, infections, or acute septic throats was the bane of all because of the lack of medicines, doctors, and hospitals. There was little hope if infection set in. One could only wait and see if nature healed the wound or wait for the end of life. Cancer was not known by that name but was called internal infection. The only way the contagious diseases could be controlled was to isolate the patient or the whole family until the illnesses subsided. Immunization and inoculations were not yet heard of in this big country.

This was a land for young, strong adults who never gave up working hard. The elderly came, a few here and there. Children died, as many as six in one family, so each parent had to plan on a large family.

In accepting this life of solitude, people became blunt toward others. They were quiet and spoke few words.

The clear, cold air brought on frisky horses, cattle, and wild animals.

Chapter XVI

Schooltime

The autumn's first cold drizzle was giving signals of winter's coming, of starting school, harvesting, and butchering time drawing near. School started in mid-September for Benny and Lea, their first year in school. Benny was nine years old and Lea was seven. Helen did not have the nerve to send her children to school at age six. It was four miles through all the unfenced prairie where wild cattle roamed, temperatures went to the extreme of fifty below, and snow was as high as the telephone posts.

On September 21, Lea's seventh birthday, Helen and Benny hitched the tamest horse, Annie, to the one-seated open buggy. Lea brought out two tin lunch boxes. While Benny handled the reins, Lea waved back to her mother until she was out of sight.

The white schoolhouse was on top of a hill. It had one room and one teacher for all eight grades. It had high, narrow windows with dark shutters on both sides of the house and one door in front. A small platform with a few steps was the entrance. The back part of the classroom had a large, round iron heating stove near the door. The students' coats and hats were hung nearby on hooks in the wall. On the side wall were crude, narrow shelves for lunch buckets. There were four rows of single seats and desks with aisles on each side and one row against the wall with double seats and desks. The tops had a slight slant, and there were deep inkwells on the sides. Below the top of the desk was an open shelf for storing tablets, books, and pencils. The seats could be turned up for recitations. The teacher's desk was long and sat on a raised platform that extended across the room. Blackboards at the end of the room on each side of the teacher's desk faced the students.

The first day in school was a traumatic experience for Benny and Lea. The English language was strange to these children, and they understood only a few essential directions. Helen had only gone to German schools. She read to her children in German, but would have to explain the text in Dutch, as that was the family language.

The teacher was trained in England and tried to be very patient. She would draw the picture of a word on the blackboard, then make Benny and Lea pronounce the word after her. She taught Lea to read and write several sentences the first day.

Lea and Benny were too bashful to play with other children at recess time. The other children teased, laughed, and poked them with sticks because they spoke a foreign language. They ate their lunch sitting in their buggy, which was parked in the school shed. Mother had instructed them how to unhitch the horse, tie it to the crib in the shed, feed it some oats and hay, then take it to the well, pump a bucket of water, and let it drink all it wanted during lunch time.

By October the winter had set in with full force. The daylight hours were few. The children started off to school when it was still dark. Helen's heart would be heavy as she saw them off each morning. She packed her children in blankets and put warm bricks in the sled. The fences along the sides of the roads were under the snow, and even the telephone poles were often covered by drifts. There was no way of opening the roads. The hope was that the horses would know the way to school, as the children could see no sign of the roads to give them directions. Helen knew that the snow was hard enough

99

to hold up the horses. Two horses were used to pull the heavy sled.

Lea and Benny took turns holding the reins so that they could warm their hands on the warmed bricks under the blankets. Their knit mittens were not wind- or snowproof. They kept their faces behind the board in the front of the low sled, as otherwise the horses would kick the snow into their faces until they could not see.

By the time they reached the schoolhouse their hands were so frozen that their fingers could not move, so the horses were unhitched and taken into the shed by hands that felt like stubs. Entering the schoolhouse, Lea and Benny aimed for the stove to warm up. The teacher saw that they could not take off their coats, so she started to help them. Both the children seemed stunned, standing silent and stiff as posts. After removing Lea's mittens, the teacher noticed her fingers sticking straight out. She sent another student out to get a basin of snow to put the children's frozen hands in so that their fingers would defrost slowly. This kept the pain of defrosting from being too bad, but it still caused severe pain. Finally the pain caused Benny and Lea to make a very faint whining sound, which was a sign of life after the shock from extreme chill. It left them too weak to concentrate on their books. After school was out, it was still blowing snow so hard it seemed as dark as night. Benny complained to Lea that he could not see the road, and he believed the horses could not even find the way home, so he turned into the first farmhouse they saw.

The farmer and his family welcomed the two small children into their warm house, gave each child a warm bedroom, and then telephoned Helen that her children were safe. They would stay for the night or until the storm was over.

In the morning the farmer's wife noticed that Lea and Benny seemed to have a fever and had a hard time holding their spoons to eat. By noon the sun came out, but the farmer decided that the children seemed too ill to drive home by themselves, as the temperature read fifty degrees below zero. He drove one team and his wife drove the other, the children bundled up in many heavy blankets.

Helen kept watching for a sight of her children's coming home. When she saw them coming, still a mile off, she ran out to meet them, leaving Rachel in her bed. To make sure she would not venture out into the cold alone, she tied her in the bed with a soft bathrobe sash.

She carried Lea in while the farmer carried Benny. Noticing that neither child could take off their mittens, Helen undressed them and put warm clothes on them. Lea's feet were so swollen, her mother had to take a sharp pair of scissors to cut the felt shoes open.

In the following days Lea's small toes swelled up, red-hot looking, until the flesh broke open. She could not walk for several weeks and then only wearing men's socks. Benny's feet did not suffer that much frostbite, as he had worn his father's rubber boots over his felt shoes.

Helen phoned the teacher at her residence to ask for some assignments for her children's schoolwork, as they would not be able to get to school for several weeks.

Hereafter Lea was susceptible to chilblains every time her feet got chilled. All her toes would get red, swell, and itch, but she was not allowed to rub or scratch them, as that would cause the toes to get sores. The only thing then was to wear very soft slippers or heavy men's socks and bathe her feet in cool, but not cold, water. Lea missed many days of school in the winters, and Mother would not let Benny go to school alone.

People in the area gave this mother all kinds of suggestions for treatment of Lea's chilblains, such as "walk barefoot in the snow." This actually made them worse, as the slightest chill on her toes caused them to get red and swollen. Another was to "stand in a fresh chip of cow dung." Grandma had a good cure.

She mixed powdered sulfur with goose grease and softly massaged it in. This acted like an antibiotic. Another suggestion was to hold Lea's feet in a pan of pure turpentine for an hour at a time.

After moving to California years later, Lea never had another sign of chilblains. However, the frostbite had left scars on her toes from her skin and flesh breaking open to the bone.

Christmas Day was one of anticipation and excitement, even though there was no Christmas tree or stocking to hang by the fireplace. Instead the prettiest and largest china plates served as their place settings on the dining table and were filled with nuts, candies, homemade cookies, and an orange, an apple, or small trinkets. The larger toys were placed on the chair in front of the china plate. Helen spent late night hours setting this all up for the morning and would be doing the farm chores and milking the cows as usual before sunrise. Lea would awake first, run down the stairs, and find the door at the bottom of the stairs locked. By the time Mother came in the house, all three children would huddle and press against the door and pound their fists as hard as they could. Lea was a great lover of dolls and knew there would be one waiting for her on her chair. Daily she lined her dolls up to count and dress them. But what she really hoped for and did not always receive, depending on the long distance shipments, was an orange. If there was no bright, round orange on her plate she would pout the rest of the day. As to candies, the children never even tried to eat the hard candies and soft chocolates were unheard of. Helen would put the untouched hard candies in a clear jar within the children's reach. It remained full for the rest of the year.

The school's Christmas celebration occurred a week before Christmas and was a community affair. There was always a large Christmas tree with handmade decorations: strings of popcorn, cookies, and sometimes dried apple rings. There were real candlesticks on little clamps to pinch onto the tree branches.

To obey fire restrictions a boy was assigned to sit behind the tree with a bucket of water. The schoolboys took turns during the evening. A long program of recitations, songs, skits, and plays was conducted by the schoolchildren. Lea, with her long yellow hair, was usually assigned to be Mary, the Mother of Jesus, holding a doll and sitting quietly in the center of the stage. After the program everyone would be very quiet and listen to sleigh bells coming up the hill. Suddenly the door would swing open wide and a large man in a Santa Claus suit and big boots emerged with loud greetings and made his way up to the tree in long strides. His burden of several large bags on his back was dropped with a thud. The board members of the school passed the packages. Everyone in the community received gifts. For Helen and her children it was a long ride and would bring them home after midnight. Many Christmas programs had to be missed by this family when the weather was too violent.

Lea was as frisky as a young colt, darting from one thing to another, always holding her head up with pride. Daily duties gave her the feeling of accomplishment. She would always ask questions and then start an argument just to hold her self-esteem. Her brother was always available to argue with and to pick on, which often turned into a real squabble or a physical scrap. When she felt she was losing she started to pinch with little fingers and twist the "gander twist" (When a gander bites, it turns and twists the flesh). If that was not enough, the vicious child bite always ended the struggle. Benny would never start a fight, but he loved to argue.

On the other hand, Lea often took a very strong motherly attitude toward her brother, and no one else dared to harm him. One time a teacher threatened to beat Benny with an inch-wide rubber strap ten times for each misspelled word on his paper in the next spelling test. Ben misspelled ten words. He was ordered to come up front onto the teacher's platform and hold out his hands in front of all the students. The schoolchildren knew that just one strike would make the palm of a hand swell up. Benny bravely held both hands out, palms up, while biting his lips. Lea flinched with her whole body each time the teacher took aim at Benny's hands. Her face and neck turned as red as her rosy cheeks, and with a fearsome, angry look in her eyes of blue she leaped onto the platform between her brother and the teacher. She screamed, "Stop hurting my brother!" The teacher stopped short with the strap in mid-air and yelled back, "Get out of the way or I will hit you, too!" Lea would not move. She looked into the teacher's face with her blue eyes' piercing scorn, her rosy cheeks flaring red. Suddenly the teacher dropped her arms to her side and walked to her desk with an angry, blushing face, not saying another word. Lea put her arms around her brother and gently led him to his desk. Benny's hands were swollen and red, he rested his forehead between his hands.

After this, Lea was determined to find a way to help her brother with his spelling, even if it meant cheating. His seat was in front of hers. She pressed very hard with the pencil as the teacher gave out the spelling words, and this left impressions on the page underneath her written words. The teacher went back to her desk, and Lea would sneak the page with the impressions to her brother before the students passed the spelling list around for correction. Lea's pencil indentations were plain for him to copy over, but the corrector never noticed it. Lea understood that Ben's speech impediment affected his reading and spelling.

Whenever there was an episode of someone getting a beating with a strap, the students got together after school and waited below the hill until the teacher and her pets had locked up the schoolhouse. Then one of the tallest boys would climb through a window and take the strap from the drawer of the teacher's desk. The students huddled close together, passing

Lea standing between brother Benny and the teacher's whipping strap

around a jackknife, and cut the strap into small pieces, then threw them into the outhouse toilet hole. The strange part of this was that the teacher never inquired about the missing strap, but one of the school board members would bring another the next day.

The boy who sat in back of Lea thought himself clever in dunking her long gold braids into his inkwell. The inkwell was a little round hole in the upper right corner with a small glass container full of ink and a small metal cover. One child was assigned to fill these inkwells every day, another had to wash the blackboards, and the next one had to clean the erasers for the blackboards. The older students swept the floors and dusted everything. The most distasteful job was sweeping the boys' and girls' outhouses.

Penmanship practice was most groaned about, and every day a perfect copy had to be handed in by the students. The first-graders had to use the old-fashioned pen quill with a loose metal point. If the point got scratchy, it splattered ink all over the page. The up and down strokes had to be perfectly even, with the ink impressions alike, and not pass the ruled lines; the ovals had to be evenly spaced. If the penmanship did not come out perfectly, there would be punishment ahead, like sweeping the toilet house.

Often Lea was awarded time to work with clay, as her penmanship, spelling, and reading were well done. The teacher took a special interest in Lea's creations and set them out on the table for display.

One morning Helen put a banana into the children's lunch boxes. It was to be a special surprise, as the sight of a banana was very unusual for these youngsters. When Lea saw the banana in her lunch box she refused to eat her lunch, claiming that it was not her lunch, so she went without eating anything. It was a long day to go without a bite, from five A.M. until seven at night.

There was a strong segregation between the British settlers and the Dutch and Germans, as each group had a strong feeling for its heritage. The children from England had more self-esteem, since the teacher was educated in England. They constantly bullied, teased, and tortured the Dutch and German-speaking children, and the teacher never punished them. The difference showed up when she planned to have a plot of garden on the school grounds. She assigned a small section to each child to work the soil and sow his own choice of seeds and promise to do his own weeding. The farmers' children felt disconcerted and rebelled, saying, "We have to always work in the gardens in our homes. We weed, dig up potatoes and knock off bugs, and feed the hogs turnips every day. We come to school to learn to read and write the English language." The teacher was really vexed and did not approach the project again.

Lea was very happy with her new revelations from reading the McGuffey reader. She lived in fantasyland when reading about the fairies helping the poor and the helpless. It gave her hope and ambition and the desire to go far away. After Lea had memorized all the Mother Goose rhymes she could get ahold of Helen decided that it was time for her to memorize the long catechism in English. The children had learned all this in German but did not understand it. Helen owned no Dutch Bibles or other books. Lea found it fascinating to know and understand what she was reading and memorizing.

One March morning the sun was making the snow sparkle like millions of diamonds. There were no clouds, just the vast blue sky meeting the white snow on the horizon. The fences and the telephone posts were all under the snow, and there were no trees, hills, or houses to form a perspective. The air felt very thin. The pent up winter hibernation was almost over.

Helen warned her children to watch out for soft snow pockets underneath the hard top crust. She felt the Chinook wind was due. The Chinook wind causes the animals to act wild, especially the horses.

After school Bernard and Lea decided to take their usual shortcut, which had a deep ravine when there was no snow. It was all filled in with snow now. They did not realize the warm wind had been blowing all day while they were in school.

They had almost crossed the ravine when the horses suddenly sank up to their bellies in the snow. They were helpless to move their legs. Benny (only nine years old) knew the trouble he had to face. He instructed his seven-year-old sister to go to the side of one horse while he took the other horse. "Lift up one leg and set it forward, then the other leg, until you have moved all four legs out of the snow and set them forward. The horse will be glad to feel it can move some," he instructed. After they did each leg six times, the horses stood up straight and snorted, as if greatly relieved to feel the bottom now. Benny and Lea hurriedly leaped into the sled. The horses bolted ahead as if wild with fear, and the children felt too exhausted to care where the horses went. They could not control the mares, as the reins were gliding loosely on the snow. They knew that the horses would eventually go home to the feeding barn. Like a thunderbolt the sled hit a big rock and tore away the harness and all connections to the sled. The pole connecting the sled, called the tongue, broke off. Benny climbed out of the sled and saw the horses far out in the field. The sudden crash had frightened them. The children composed themselves to figure out their plight. There was nothing else to do but start walking. The horses were already out of sight; the snow was heavy with dampness and up above their knees. The wind started to blow hard against them, and Lea started to stumble. Her short legs could not carry her any farther. Benny looked back and saw his sister lying in the snow. He feared that she had fainted, as she had been falling into a faint of late whenever she exerted herself.

He took her by her hands and pulled her body along as if she were a sled.

In the meantime Helen saw the horses run into the corral at high speed and knew that something had happened to her children and the sled. It was getting dark, so she lit all the lamps and lanterns and put them in the windows so the children could see where the house was.

When Benny saw the light he shouted out to Lea, "We are almost home!" Helen could see a small figure in the white snow, moving very slowly, and ran out to meet him. She picked up Lea, and her other arm was soon around Benny, almost carrying him, too. Inside by the fire she changed their clothes and rubbed their small bodies until their circulation had come back, and soon they were both fast asleep.

Lea always remembered this as the longest walk of her life. Her school often seemed a hundred miles away to her. Very often in her dreams in the long midwinter nights she would invent an idea to make those miles to school easier to conquer. She dreamed she would climb up the barn roof and, as she started to jump off, her arms would flap like birds' wings and she could fly over the fields to the top of the school hill.

In April when the days were longer the children arose with the sun. They would start off early enough so that they could dawdle along. If it looked like rain, they would take the buggy. Rains did not come often, but the winds were always there to dry things fast. They had no raincoats, and sometimes they would take the table oilcloths to use as umbrellas.

The heavy grass stubble made it impossible to feel the pleasure of going barefoot in the few warm days of summer.

On their way to school the children played games with the prairie dogs by trying to beat them to their holes. The slow-moving badger was an easy chase. Badgers had a bad habit of digging holes in the middle of the road where the horses would step into them and break their legs. The children would fill these holes. The coyotes would be out looking for food. The porcupine was the one animal for which they showed respect, as they did not want to be sprayed with his quills. Often Benny would have to pull the quills out of his dog's lips.

The long summer evenings were taken up with playing out until dark. There was no outside light to spoil the brightness of the stars above. If the evenings were warm enough, the children would lie on the grass counting the falling stars. The one who saw the most stars was awarded a sweet biscuit. The northern lights brought as big a thrill as the appearance of a rainbow. There was no special rainy season, just once in a while a quick thundershower. The bright blue skies had few clouds, and when the clouds did show up, the children spent a lot of time seeing faces and imagining designs in the fairylands. Running barefoot in mud puddles after a shower brought out squeals and screams.

There never was any thought of swimming; bathing suits were unheard of. At Grandma's creek it was too cold and the water was too strong and swift for children to wade in.

On warm spring days the students who went westward from school would walk home. They traveled together because of the danger in crossing that part of the prairie. To take the shortest way home they would go across the unfenced part of the prairie, where the wild cattle and horses roamed. After crawling under the heavy barbed-wire fence, each one would stop, look, and listen for any cattle in the distance. If there was any group of stampeding cattle coming their way, they could hear it on the ground. At the same time, if the people were too many or noisy with their footsteps, the cattle would feel the vibrations and come in a stampede.

The children could not see any cattle around, so they continued on. As they got almost to the other end of the field a rumbling started in a thick dust, where dark forms seemed almost upon them. The youngsters all ran as fast as their feet could go, and Lea, being the smallest, was behind while trying to run as fast as her short legs could go. The older boys called to her to drop her red sweater, thinking the cattle could see red first. By the time they reached the fence by the road, they looked around and saw the leader bull stomping the red sweater into the ground and throwing it into the air until it tore in many pieces. After Lea had dropped her sweater, the oldest boy picked her up and carried her the rest of the way. Their last sight of the cattle was of each animal taking a turn at part of the sweater, as if that were the best sport in the world.

The boys cheered at their victorious escape, but Lea's tears rolled down her cheeks at the loss of her red sweater. The fourteen-year-old boy who carried her to safety was her hero thereafter.

Another nice early spring day the same group took another route toward a small creek which the cattle usually did not jump over. Just as the herd came roaring toward them, the boys reached the creek and jumped over. Lea just stood beside the water, looking down and knowing she could not jump that far. When she hesitated, a steer that did not have matured horns pushed her from behind into the water and her lunch bucket flew off into the water. She stood in the middle of the stream up to her knees watching her bucket sail off, screaming, "My bucket, my bucket!" She had made a picture of a cat out of sandpaper that said at the bottom. "Scratch my back" to be hung by the stove for lighting matches. She had put that into her bucket, and though she was not hurt physically, she felt deep remorse over the loss of the gift for her mother.

Chapter XVII

Home

The home atmosphere stays with a child into adulthood, and pleasant and unpleasant family affairs are passed down to the next generation. Lea vowed to herself when still very young to try to remember only the good things and to pass them on to her own family but never let the same unpleasant things happen to her children if she could prevent it. Her feeling was that the less the unpleasant was talked about, the sooner it would be forgotten. She trained her mind to always look at the silver lining of the dark clouds. This helped her to smile in sorrow or in pain, so she was always taken for a happy person.

Benny, Lea, and Rachel needed a father but had no knowledge of a father's place in the home. They were so isolated that there was not much association with other families. A father gives the children the security of a full family. He is someone to follow. A father is someone to pull the child out of a mud hole and instill in the child the courage to face his future. These young ones did feel that something was missing in their lives, but since they did not know any better, they were happy and very active. They often begged Mother to buy the hired man for their father.

Five years after the death of her husband, Helen had all the debts paid and was now making a profit from her farm. She leased most of the land to other farmers to grow wheat and oats, but kept enough land to graze her cows and horses. She

The Piner farm in 1918, homesteaded in 1902

sold the milk she did not need to the cheese factory. It was picked up by a person with a large wagon who went to all the farmers in the area. Helen got cash for each ten-gallon galvanized can full of milk. Her best profit was in raising pigs. After the piglets were fattened up and ready for market, she would have them taken to the railroad station and shipped them to Calgary. She then would take the same train and sell her pigs to her favorite merchants. She would "do" the city for several days and sometimes for a week. The children stayed home alone but did not have school. The hired man did the heavy chores but did not have to live with them.

To the children it was like Christmas, as they looked forward to having their mother come home bringing all kinds of goodies and clothes for them. She left with a list of each child's needs. Their wants were few, except Lea always wanted another doll and another picture book and Benny always wanted a new carving knife. Rachel was content to share with her sister, but she always got the same as Lea did. With great pride Helen would bring many boxes, plus the rolls of fresh money which were to last for another year.

Helen was always very economical and a wise businesswoman. She could make do financially on the same income others found impossible.

With her garden and chickens, their diet was well balanced except for a lack of fruit. Sauerkraut was the only source of vitamin C available. She sewed and made all the clothes except shoes. She drew diagrams of the children's feet and sent them to the Eaton catalog or took the measurements with her on her yearly trip to the city. Seldom did the shoes fit right, but they had to wear them just the same.

The community talk was that the young widow's children were the best dressed of all around. They had more toys, dolls, and picture books and were the best fed. Her children took very good care of everything they had and never broke their toys. If something did break accidently, it was repaired.

Helen studiously learned to read and speak English along with her children. The McGuffey primer was memorized along with verses from the English version of the Bible. The Mother Goose rhyme books and the fairy tales about the kings and queens were the fun books for them all. The German newspaper from Winnipeg, Manitoba, was tossed away and forgotten. There was no other newspaper or magazine available. Now the long catechism and the Ten Commandments had to be memorized in English as well.

Life on the farm was a daily rhythm of keeping alive. The spirit of cooperation was as strong in the animals as in each person. The dogs, cats, and horses had their chores also. Life was like constantly pumping well water giving life to all.

The winter months and days seemed long, starting in September, until in June at four o'clock in the afternoon the sun would hide its face behind the majestic Rocky Mountains while the other three sides of the Alberta prairies ran off into the horizon.

All the chores were finished an hour after dark and the stock settled for a long night's sleep. The hired man went off to his own home.

The kitchen cook stove was within a few feet and was fed with hard coal. On the stove a large kettle of water steamed all the time. In the back part there was a pot of wheat cooking for their breakfast and a pot of stew for the next day. They made a tempting scent in the air. Once a week, baking bread brought a delightful aroma.

The children had to do extra homework to make up for the days of school they missed. For recess Helen taught the little girls to sew, knit, and crochet, while Benny settled down to whittle, letting the shavings drop into the coal bucket.

Lea hated to knit her long socks or stockings, as they were called. She always complained that they made her skin itch, but she loved to crochet fancy lace for her petticoats and nightgowns. Helen lined the fancy caps Lea crocheted to wear as dust caps or nightcaps.

To prepare for bed each child slipped a heavy flannel nightgown over his woolen underwear and was given a heated brick wrapped in a towel. They marched up the narrow stairs holding a tiny three-inch kerosene lamp. The one room upstairs was not heated. The mattresses were homegrown wheat straw filled into a striped heavy ticking cloth. Another soft mattress was filled with goose feathers, and there was the same size feather comforter to cover up with. One sank in so deep that his small head could not be seen. Thus they all kept warm even in forty or fifty degrees below zero. Getting out of bed was the most unpleasant thing of all. Each bed had a large heavy china pot for the necessary nature's relief. The clacking sound of covering up the pot with the lid would arouse everyone, and then each person had to do his own clacking.

Arising time came when they heard Helen stoking the stove, shaking out the ashes, and carrying them out in buckets. Benny took the milk buckets to the barn by climbing over the high snowdrifts, as Lea started breakfast by making the Postum of ground roasted wheat and other grains. In the barn the stock made all the noise they could, asking for food. Benny gave each animal a forkful of hay, while Helen gave each one a bucket of grain. The cats came scampering under and around the cows' and horses' feet to demand their food, feeling that it was their privilege for having spent the night chasing the mice. When Helen started to milk, the cats heard the squirting sound of the milk against the pail when she pulled the cows' teats. This was music to the cats; six of them would settle close by waiting for their ration of milk. Helen was always very quiet, but Benny liked to whistle, although he knew no tunes of any songs. The dog was still lying lazily with one eye open, watching the activities. The horses did not like the cats near their feet, so they would kick the cats out of the way, often stepping on them and crippling or killing them.

The pigs and the chickens each had a small shed.

The dog was a good watchdog and shepherd. He knew when it was time to bring the cows in from the pasture. He knew too which was the milk cow to bring home. He watched for wild predators and would give them a chase. If a calf or young colt, chicken, or pig got out of its pen, he would corner it and keep barking until some person came to take over. He also knew when a stranger like a hunter or gypsy came around and let out a ferocious growl. He would not let anyone get closer than five feet to any family member until Helen or Benny would hush him up.

Neither the cats nor the dog ever came into the house, except one big tomcat, the king of the cat population, whose job was to keep the mice out of the cellar and the house. The cellar door was in the middle of the kitchen floor and had to be lifted up in order to walk into the cellar. The top of the cellar door was the same as the rest of the kitchen floor. The old tomcat was so huge and strong that he could push up the door even after they put some chairs or a table on top. To the children it was a great sport to let the cat push them up even with all three sitting on the door. Helen had tried to do away with this cat, but he seemingly had more than one life, as he kept coming back.

Two horses were used to pull the low, long sled made of boards and to pull the bigger buggy. The one-seater sled and the one-seat buggy used only one horse.

The pigs often caused some mischief, like digging holes under their fence and escaping to dig holes in the garden. The chickens were free as birds, because there was no fence for them. Some of the hens would wander away from the barn in the early

117

The large cat pushing up the cellar door while the children sit on it

spring and come back several weeks later with a surprise of six little chicks or more. The cows were strictly for milk, butter, and cheese. They were the most stupid of all animals; when getting out of the pasture fence they could not find their way back. When the ground was covered with snow the cows would not dig through the snow for the grass, while the horses scraped the snow off until they got to the grass. When the farm stock became ill or injured or too old, the usual thing was to kill and bury them in some unused corner of the field, as there was no veterinarian in the area. It was considered inhumane to allow an animal to suffer, although there were many home remedies used for ordinary belly bloating.

One day the old horse that took the children to school, Annie, reached too far over the fence and got her foot caught in the barbed wire. The harder she tried to free the foot, the deeper the wire cut, until she could not move at all. She kept neighing and whinnying until Benny heard her. The dog had been barking and the other horses came over and the cows stood around with curiosity. Soon the whole family was helping to free Annie's foot. Helen brought a wire cutter. Old Annie had lost much blood and had fallen down. They washed and dressed the wound, wrapped the horse with blankets, and gave her water to drink out of a bottle. The children stayed with old Annie all night, soothing her and rubbing her back. In the morning Helen called an old farmer to come and look at the horse. After he examined the wound, he said, "Old Annie will have to be shot, as her foot will never be useful again." The children cried and begged that she be let live so that they could take good care of her. They took turns staying with their horse for a week. Then, on a sunny day, she arose and put her weight on the foot. She was able to go to the school again, even though she had a limp for the rest of her very long life. After all, the children did not need a horse for speed.

Every summer Helen sent her children to summer school where the German language was taught. She wanted them to learn another language in addition to English. This school was in another district, but only two miles away. It was a fun school, lasting only half a day and holding most classes outdoors. Eating lunch outside was a daily picnic. The school had no well water tank or trough. Lea would jump on old Annie bareback with just a rope around the horse's neck and race the others to water.

One time old Annie stepped into a hole, as she was rather clumsy with her lame foot. As the horse lunged down in front she threw Lea over her head and under her forefeet and stepped on Lea's chest, which winded her. Lea lay in the grass without moving, and the old horse walked around her until the teachers arrived. They feared that her chest must be crushed, as they could see the hoof marks on it. While the teachers talked about the problem, Lea got up to fetch her horse. Old Annie showed concern and was relieved as Lea came to her. They all decided that the horse must have been aware that Lea was under her foot and had stepped very lightly, not putting her full weight on that foot.

Once in a while Lea, Benny, and Rachel would go to an uncle's farm several miles away and have fun playing with cousins. One of their favorite games was to let out the big ram. The ram acted like the king of all. He would come bearing down on anyone in front of him with his head down and horns aiming toward the person. The children would stand near a big tree and wait for him to get near them, then quickly jump aside behind the tree. The sheep could not stop in time and would hit his horns into the tree. He would shake his head as if stunned. This brought out a gay laugh from the youngsters. The ram would not give up. He would back away with a bellow and come toward them with more determination than ever.

This would go on until the farmhand sent the sheep back into the corral with the help of a sheepdog.

Old Annie's second daughter was now old enough to be trained to carry a rider and pull the buggy. Benny tried to hitch her up, but she did not like the harness, deciding to kick her hind legs and hitting him square in his face. She knocked out several of his teeth and cut open his upper lip. After some time new teeth grew in, but they were not even or straight, this without a dentist's ever seeing Benny's teeth.

At nine years old Lea managed the kitchen well, getting up with Benny and Helen to cook breakfast while they did the outdoor chores. The cookstove was too high for her to reach the big pots. She had to invent ways to lift them. One morning while lifting the big teakettle full of boiling water—it was too heavy to hold up, so she leaned it on the two-quart coffeepot— the whole kettle of hot water fell on her legs and thighs. Good luck was hers when Benny and her mother walked in. Helen set her buckets of milk down and ordered Benny to take the stocking off one leg while she took off the other. The burning pain left Lea in shock; she did not realize what had happened. Helen carried her into the living room, put her on the sofa, and then took ice cold linens and put them on Lea's legs as she was now starting to scream. Helen then called the doctor.

The doctor directed Helen to put petroleum jelly on the red spots and, after the blisters formed, take a silk thread and needle and take the thread through the blisters, leaving the thread hanging down at each end. That would make the fluid leak out slowly and the skin lie down thus letting the blistered skin form a skin graft. Lea's legs became full of large blisters all close together. After she was bedfast for six weeks, her skin was growing together, but she walked very bowlegged, as the skin was still very tight.

The schoolteacher was very kind and sent Lea assignments, some clay, and picture books. Lea started school when she was

121

still bowlegged, and the other students teased and mocked her. She was so very happy to be able to walk again that she ignored the teasing. After several years no scars were left.

While Lea was convalescing, Aunt Anita came to show Lea how to crochet, knit, and embroider. She was constantly doing something, plus reading a lot, but she did have a lot of time to stare up at the ceiling, where the plaster was cracking and spotted, and she imagined all kinds of pictures. The frosted window was her best palette, where she designed fields, trees, and mountains.

When Lea and Rachel played tea party their mother showed them how to pour tea, hold the cups like ladies, with their little fingers pointing bluntly out, and take bites of cookies like English ladies. They would cross their legs or sit with their knees close together.

Helen taught her girls to be clean housekeepers. The cracks in the wide floorboards had to be brushed, and with a hairpin every particle of dust had to be removed. She did not expect her daughters to milk the cows, as that was not for ladies. She had great hopes for them to marry well-to-do men. As for the arts, she had no knowledge of them and considered pictures, dancing, and music unnecessary evils. Lea always kept her desire for the dance, painting, or music to herself.

Benny and Rachel went out to the large pasture where they saw the old condemned well. As Rachel was very thirsty, she reached into the shallow well to get a dipper of water to drink. The next morning she awoke with a very high fever and a stomachache. This was diagnosed as typhoid fever, which in those days usually meant death. Rachel's platinum blond hair all started to fall out a handful at a time. She was very thin and weak and could not eat anything. After the fever came down, she was so very hungry that she would take a little crumb from the table very slowly and raise her hand to get it to her mouth.

In several weeks her new hair started to come in and it was much darker.

*   *   *

Before the Russian civil war a deal was made with the Netherlands for some Dutch citizens to go to show the Russians how to grow hard wheat, which makes the best flour for bread. The Dutch became very prosperous and built large estates and owned a lot of farmland. The revolutionaries started to take over the country by torturing the wealthy people, ruining their property, hanging them, and chopping off the heads of even women and children, so many people escaped to Canada and America. These immigrants would come to visit and tell the violent stories. While Lea was supposed to sleep she could hear them up the stairway. She wept and prayed to God, "Please, God, do not let those Bolsheviks come over here."

We may not always see or know how the weaving of a child's life will develop, but one day the canvas will unroll and show that dark days are of a value, as dark colors on a canvas bring out the light colors and improve the scene.

Benny was given a beautiful riding pony for his birthday. He made a firm rule that no one else was to ride his horse. Grandpa gave him a special new saddle. Lea's temptation was very strong, and she constantly watched for a chance to sneak on the pony's back. One afternoon her opportunity arrived: she saw Benny tie the horse near the house but leave the reins of the bridle hanging loose as he came in to get a snack. Swiftly she slithered around the corner, patted the pony's head, and put her foot into the stirrups of the saddle, and the second she settled on the saddle the pony reared up on its hind legs. The pony was aware that she was not Benny. She was not prepared for this sudden overthrow and landed with the middle of her back on the rough fence post.

Benny found his sister hanging over the fence like a big lump. He pulled her off and proceeded to shake her body to make her breathe. When she finally opened her eyes, the first thing she did was beg Benny not to tell Mother. "I do not want her punishment," she said. He could see that his sister was really hurt, as she could not move without pain, but he promised not to tell. Several days later her mother asked Lea to pick something off the floor, but Lea just stood there without saying a word. Finally she mumbled, "I cannot bend over; it hurts." Helen kept quizzing Lea until she had told all, and Benny sneaked out very silently.

The only thing Helen could think of was to take Lea to a neighbor who was an unlicensed chiropractor. After examining Lea's back, he claimed her spine was injured and because of waiting so long for treatment it had started to grow that way and it was too late to correct it. He said she would have more problems if any corrections were attempted.

Rachel and Benny spent a lot of time playing and doing chores outdoors while Lea did all the indoor work. Rachel pretended to be a tomboy, wearing boys' clothes even though it was taboo to wear them. She was daring when it came to being with the boys, but to her mother she was the darling of the family. Her mother could never imagine that Rachel could do any mischief. The men in the field teased Rachel a lot. One time they coaxed her to take a bit of chewing tobacco, so she took up the dare and went on to play. As she was jumping off a haystack she accidently swallowed the whole piece. Her face turned as green as grass, and she had an upset stomach for days. She liked to play with snakes, the small harmless ones mostly, to tease Lea. She would let several snakes go up her arms and neck. This would anger Lea very much and she would spank her sister, but to Rachel it was all a happy game.

Chapter XVIII

At Grandma's House

In 1917 at the beginning of America's involvement in World War I, life was unpleasant for non-British immigrants, as the British-born acted antagonistically toward foreign-speaking people. This caused the schoolchildren to behave the same way. Since Lea and Benny were the youngest, they were harassed the most. Their lunches were taken away and thrown in the toilet hole. The horse's harnesses were cut into many pieces, or the buggy was rolled down the hill to break the hitch or axle. The small children were beaten with broomsticks, but they never even let out a cry. The teachers were transferred frequently, and those of British heritage never did stop these violent actions by the students, if they were aware of them. This left a mark in Lea's mind for her lifetime. Whenever Lea saw a person being persecuted, no matter what color, creed, or nationality, it would break her heart until her dying day.

World War I ended in 1918, and the soldiers came home, bringing with them the flu epidemic. Many people were so ill that they could not take care of their own farms. The well ones had to help out. The schools and the churches closed and were used as hospitals. Many people died, and the well people kept burying the dead without any witnesses. The children had to stay at home, and yet it seemed the flu was more of an adult disease. The soldiers who had lived through the war became very ill, and many died. The people who lived through this epidemic held memorial services for the ones that had gone when the epidemic was over with in late spring.

Helen volunteered to take care of the farm nearest her place. She milked the many cows and left the buckets full of milk by the door of the sick family. She fed the hogs, chickens, and horses and then walked home to do her own chores. Before she entered her house she made a complete change of clothes so that she would not bring any germs to her children. For a month she trudged back and forth in the bitter cold.

Grandma and Grandpa came to see if they could help and took Lea back with them. The three uncles at Grandma's insisted on eating all the baked onions they could eat. The oven was constantly baking dozens of onions, and someone was always sitting in front of the stove. They claimed eating these onions would keep the flu away. They chased Lea all around trying to convince her to eat them. She found a good place to keep out of their reach under Grandma's bed in the far corner of her room. Grandpa's cure was to drink a lot of sauerkraut juice.

Grandma taught Lea to peel apples with as long and thin a skin as possible without breaking it. She was given a bright colored ribbon for her hair for each long length of apple peeling. Grandma spent a lot of time combing and braiding Lea's hair, while calling her bright yellow hair "a head of gold." It was not easy for the spirited young girl to sit still to have her long hair combed and braided. When not braided, her hair came below her seat. It would always get tangled in with the wicker chair tops, and when she ran through the low trees and bushes she would feel she like she was being hung up alive. She left many wads of hair behind her, but at least when her hair got a tight braiding it did not have to be combed every day. Her hairbrush was made of hundreds of straight pins with the sharp ends cut off, the only type of brush that took the tangles out. When the style of bobbing the hair came in Lea would beg

Mother and Grandma to cut her hair, but they would not give in to her.

One Christmas school program Lea was to sit in the front of the stage with her yellow hair hanging down, holding a doll. The family came home after midnight, and everyone was too tired to comb and braid her hair. In the morning her mother worked and worked to get her tangled hair combed and caused a lot of tears of pain for Lea. Suddenly Mother took the scissors and hacked off most of the hair. To the young girl all the tears paid off; now she was like the other girls.

Summertime was always a long time coming and only lasted for two short months. The month of May sometimes had nice days in which to plant the garden. June was a pleasant time to walk to school, and the four miles did not seem too long.

Every summer there was an annual ice-cream feast, when Grandma would mix a lot of eggs with fresh cream, vanilla, and sugar. The men chipped ice off the big blocks in the icehouse. There would be as many as six freezers being turned when the whole clan turned up for this. Someone always brought some wild strawberries and some cookies came with it, but nothing else was served, for everyone was determined to eat enough ice cream to last until next year. People ate all afternoon until dark.

On some Easters there would be nice weather and the snow would be partially gone. There was no school on Good Friday, and Helen would be baking all kinds of rolls, breads, and cookies. She would send the children to go on an adventure to the creek, filling their buckets with rolls and cookies. The water in the creek was very clean and cold. The first thing they did was take off their shoes and stockings and attempt to go wading, but the water was too cold to really walk in.

All three children behaved like young wild colts. Bernard would look for willow twigs to make bows and arrows; his only target was the snowbank. Returning to the house feeling tired and hungry, they smelled fresh baked bread and buns and they hoped Mother would have their supper ready. She had scrubbed the house, and the kitchen floor felt perfect to stretch out on.

Whenever Benny was threatened by severe punishment he would sneak out of the house with his blanket wrapped around his waist. He ran to the nearest group of bushes miles away. When darkness came he would see all kinds of animals peering at him while he sat huddled with his blanket. Then he would see the eyes of the lynx looking down on him. They seemed to him as bright as a flashlight, and with the speed of lightning Benny's legs brought him home. Mother never worried about his being out; she knew how afraid he was of his imaginary lynx, and besides, there was nothing to be afraid of. At the same time Lea sat in a corner covering her face with her arms and praying for the safety of her brother.

Something new and wonderful came to this community. New telephone poles were being set in the ground along the side of the road. The children found a new entertainment for themselves; by putting their ears against the big posts they heard all kinds of whistles and ringing. The girls picked up the green glass insulators which were shaped like drinking tumblers and used them for dishes to play house. Lea dressed them up to look like dolls.

One bright summer Sunday morning Helen dressed her two daughters (six and eight years old) in new white shoes and stockings, newly made pink flowered dresses, and white Panama hats trimmed with bright ribbons like a couple of peacocks. The shoes were only of canvas, but it was their white color that dazzled. It was a dusty walk, and when they got within sight of the church, a group of rough boys jumped up at them from a small creek, throwing blobs of mud on the white outfits. The frightened sisters ran back home without stopping until they got there. Their faces were all dirty with tears and dust. The boys had also called them "the dirty widow's children," which the young girls could not understand. What was bad about being a widow's child? Also, they were teased about being the rich widow's girls. Helen was a good seamstress and dressed her family well, and she managed the farm perfectly, with a profit almost every year.

Helen had a suitor, a widower in the neighborhood who would come calling often in the late evening after the children were in bed. Every time he came to spend the late hours talking and talking in the kitchen, Helen would end up sobbing in bed the rest of the night. Lea, sharing the bed with her mother, was also disturbed. Her young mind could not reason it out and was puzzled about this man making her mother cry. She began to hate this man coming to the house.

Helen had a brother living a day's drive by buggy from Grandma's house, and he asked if Lea would come to stay a month or so in the summer to play or baby-sit with his four daughters, all under five years old. The four miles to her grandparents' house seemed a slow ride with the mare Annie and her limp. They left early in the morning, when the sunrise turned everything gold. They had to cross the river, which had no bridge, and the water was high enough to reach the buggy seat. Old Annie had to swim and pull the buggy at the same time, as she could not reach the bottom of the river. Lea was begging, "Oh, Annie, please do not let us drown here." The old horse knew what to do and did not need to be whipped onward. But Lea felt that Annie needed to be encouraged. The rest of the way was a long, dusty road, not one house in view. When they reached their destination at sundown, their clothes were caked with mud from the dust and the river water.

Helen went home the next morning, and Lea ran after her mother for a mile, crying to go back with her. For a ten-year-old she did her job very well, entertaining the children all day long. It was a very lonely time for her. She had no privacy to take a bath or to sleep, as she shared the one bedroom with the family. There was no one to talk to, as this aunt and uncle didn't seem the talking type. The loneliness spoiled her appetite and her sleep. There was no sound of cattle, dogs, or coyotes to be heard, only one rooster and a few chickens. There was no tree or bush for a bird to live in, no road for passersby or a telephone, not even a pole. However, there was one big rock not far from the house where she spent most of the time, helping the little girls to climb onto it and then jump off into her arms. Her mother had braided Lea's hair very tight, and she had no hairbrush to comb it. She had just a small basin to wash in and no well water nearby.

Her uncle announced that he would drive her to her grandmother's house the next day after the month's stay. Lea's eyes brightened, and a silent joy crossed her tired, thin face when she saw the outline of her grandparents' farm even before crossing the river.

The yard was filled with many buggies with the horses still hitched. She went among them looking for old Annie, but instead she noticed a most peculiar vehicle she'd never seen before. Her uncle behind her said, "That's an auto." She just stood and stared at the big, black, shiny painted thing. Her mother suddenly appeared, hugging her very affectionately, which puzzled the girl, as it was not like her mother to show so much emotion. Helen put her hand on Lea's head and felt her braids, then whipped out a hairbrush from her heavy skirt pocket, remarking, "Your hair needs washing." As she pulled the steel pin brush through Lea's hair, big bunches of hair came with it. This so touched Helen's emotions that she let her tears roll down her face, holding her daughter close to her and saying, "What has happened to you? Your rosy cheeks and your round face are gone."

They were sitting on the fender of the black monster, and Lea kept looking up at it. Helen pointed at it and said, "This contraption is a car that belongs to the man that I am going to marry. He will be your stepfather. He is the same man that used

130

to come and see me often." Lea could only think of how her mother would weep all night long after he visited her. She was so startled all she could yell out was, "Why?" following with a whispered "I do not feel good," and she fainted, sliding down onto the ground. Helen carried her indoors, and she felt that Lea was very light and thin. She came in to her grandma's bed; her mother was giving her some odd-tasting stuff which she recognized as Grandma's homemade wine. When Grandma came in the room, Helen quickly left without speaking to her. Grandma seemed very angry, as she always mumbled to herself when she was angry. Now she kept saying to herself, "I told her that if she married that no-account drinking man I would not speak to her again." Lea then went to sleep and awoke with silence all around her. All the people were gone and it was dark when Grandma came in reporting that everyone had left. She told Lea she was to stay here until she regained her strength.

The adult people did not exhibit their sentimental emotions. There were seldom any happy greetings with kisses and hugs and not much laughter. Angry words were kept silent also. The children learned to watch for signs in outward behavior, like Grandma would mumble to herself, Grandpa would sputter but never get his words out, and Helen would give the person she was angry with a week of the silent treatment.

Grandma would show her moods well enough. She was a very calm, casual, friendly, and talkative person, and when it came to flowers and plants her house was full of flowers and she could keep flowers blooming all winter long. In summer her garden looked like a formal English garden with beds in all-sized circles. She had taught herself to read English by reading the seed catalogs, and she spoke three other languages, German, Dutch, and Russian. When a preacher came to her house and accused her of spending too much time on her flowers and telling her there would be no flowers in heaven, she answered, "Then I do not want to go to heaven." In the

131

evening after cooking for the five hardworking men, she would take time out for a short happy trip down to the cellar to have a nip of her homemade wine. Grandma would pretend to cull out the apples, and if Lea was there she had her pick the bad apples out of the barrel and in return gave Lea a bedtime story.

When September came around it was taken for granted that Lea must go back to school. She had not forgotten her mother's statement about getting married and shuddered at the thought of it, not wanting to go home. She did not know that this would be her last stay with her grandparents.

When Grandpa had hitched the horses to the two-seater with the black top, Grandma stated that she would not come along. It was a beautiful autumn day, so the ride did not seem too long. Arriving near her mother's farm, Lea noticed something different. On reaching the yard, she saw a new house going up next to the small cottage. She was not expecting such a drastic change this soon. Her daydreams were always about something new, but that her mother would remarry had never entered her thoughts.

Helen explained to her father that she had to make more space, as her husband-to-be had four boys and three girls. Grandpa also knew that she had to pay for all this, as Mr. Freeling had a very big debt and no way of paying it off.

The three children felt very frustrated and could not understand this new life to come—what it would be like to have a strange man as head of the household and so many more people to live with—but Helen was too busy to notice that her children felt so troubled. Rachel seemed young enough to be happy about the change to come, but Benny and Lea became more and more unsociable and began to hide when strange men came to build the new house.

After finding her children sobbing and huddled together in a corner, Helen explained that it would take all winter to finish the house.

Helen confided to her father, "James promised me he would never drink again. I know he will try and then fail. I hope I can encourage him to keep trying to stop his drinking. He is kind and good to me. I feel very strongly about feeding and clothing neglected children. It's my mission to help this family."

Her father left with a warning: "To take on a big family for pity will bring you costly problems." Stepping onto his buggy, he mumbled, "This man has made promises before and is too weak to keep them."

Mr. James Frank Freeling was always friendly and kind and had a special feeling of sympathy toward the sick and people in pain. He was always doing something to help the suffering. He was not strong on religion but liked philosophy, which he always studied or read. He had taught himself to read in several languages before starting grade school. He was self-supporting at fifteen years old, working as a clerk in a general store. He became a salesman for farm machinery in Winnipeg, but came to Didsbury to get a job making doors. He organized and managed a cheese factory to help the farmers get extra cash. When the area needed a post office he volunteered to be the first postmaster. He learned to set the broken legs of the animals and progressed to setting broken bones for people. He was called "the unlicensed chiropractor" on the prairie.

He had a way of rubbing a patient's back, neck, or leg muscles with a tender, delicate massage that made the whole body relax. He was acquainted with every vertebra in the spine and all bone connections. He would feel for any injured, out-of-place bone connection while massaging, and the person would not be aware of his setting the bone straight. While massaging he would have the patient sit backward on the chair and lean his head back on the chair or sometimes the person would lie on a plain bench. He was called a miracle maker, but he never asked for a cent. Often the farmers brought him farm or garden produce.

One day he saw an ad in the Winnipeg newspaper about a dental kit. Two months later it arrived in a small box with tools to pull teeth and fill teeth with quicksilver. Many people came to him with toothaches.

He was always going from one job to another. He never asked for money and would lose jobs because of his desire for whiskey. He even taught school for a year and was relieved by Ben Piner, Helen's first husband, for being too drunk during school session.

There was never enough to feed his seven children. He was no gardener, nor a farmer. The neighbors always helped the family.

Mr. Freeling was never seen to be angry, but was very affectionate and kind. When he was drunk he was even friendlier. He was capable of doing many things, but he could not earn money or keep it.

It was his whiskey problem that disturbed Mr. and Mrs. Abe Loen, Helen's parents.

Lea missed her grandmother very much. She was constantly scanning the road for a surrey with a black top, remembering her grandma stepping down, putting her hands under her big apron, and pulling out sugar lumps. Lea's favorite was a box of Grandma's molasses cookies.

Occasions to send Lea to stay with Grandma never arose again.

Chapter XIX

Three Frustrated Children

Jack, Helen's younger brother, came to visit the family. Seeing that the three children were in need of cheering up, he started to tell about a trip to the Calgary city fair.

"I saw seven elephants, just like the ones in your storybooks. Their long, flexible snouts would swing from side to side keeping time with the band music, and the ivory tusks looked white and shiny. Their fat, short legs are attached to big feet, walking as soft as your cat. But their skin looks wrinkled, tough, and dirty gray." By this time he had the children's attention, and their eyes were wide open.

"On the street was a thing that looked like a square tub. A man was turning a wheel which started some music. It is called a hurdy-gurdy. The wheels inside rubbed together, making a sound like a flute.

"Then I took a ride on an airplane, the first time I had seen one. It had two wide wings on each side. I was the only passenger. It was very cold and windy. I had to hang onto my cap with one hand and hold onto the seat with the other. The airplane turned around and around, then upside down. It's called the loop-de-loop. I was so nervous and excited that I wet my pants."

This last part created hilarious, unrestrained laughter, especially as the uncle acted out the airplane story.

Uncle Jack telling stories about the Calgary City Fair to cheer up the three children

Uncle Jack was very active and interested in sports like skating and hockey. He was a body builder, always lifting heavy weights and flexing his muscles. He was always game for adventure. Recently he had organized a baseball group after having tried boxing with his own boxing mitts. "I socked him good, but when I get some bought boxing gloves I will win the fight," he said.

To these children this uncle was their hero. Uncle Jack had never been ill, not even with a cold, and seemed immune to all the epidemics that came around every year. He was fussy about eating the right foods.

Putting his arm around all three children, he said, "Let's go eat some of your mother's hodgepodge stew. It will take away your hiccups."

The big basement of the new house being built was finished. The big beams in the walls were waiting for the side boards. The builders were up on top putting on the roof. Lea walked down the new steps, looking around and wondering what would go into this area. While she was looking up, something flew into her right eye. She worked all evening trying to get the irritant out of the eye. Helen hitched the one-horse buggy and went for the doctor, who was a full hour away. The doctor put such strong medicine in Lea's eye that it caused her to scream and roll on the floor. She was to keep the eye bandaged and put the strong medicine on it once a day. Needless to say, she lost half the sight of her eye.

Benny found himself a foot-long two-by-four, a beam from the house being built. He settled himself in his hideaway to carve out a doll for his sister Lea. After two weeks of isolating himself, he brought his treasure, hiding it under his jacket, to Lea. She looked it over and was amazed. She stroked the smooth body of the doll with her mouth wide open, then, holding it at arm's length, tried the movements of the arms and legs; it had elbows and knees, too. She held it against her body, then kissed the smooth little head. It was the treasure of her life. Every day the sister and brother would sit close together on the stair steps talking about his creation. He would explain in detail how he made the legs and arms, how often one would break and then he would start another. He showed how he smoothed each part with his knife as he had no sanders or sandpaper. Both agreed to name it Wooden Peter.

A teenager of the Freeling family had watched this daily toy conversation between the sister and brother. He came up to them and grabbed the wooden creation, growling, "Let me see it," then dropped it between the inside and outside walls, and it slipped with a rattle between the two-by-fours. The teenager ran off. Lea wept as if her heart would break. Benny quietly went to find some wire, and until dark the two children tried to catch the doll with a stiff wire, but never could get a hook onto the lost treasure.

Lea (ten years old) did get a brainstorm of an idea. She wanted to give her mother a surprise birthday party in the hope that she could get Grandma to come over and love her mother again. She checked her memory of the ingredients of a cake Grandma had taught her, which were one egg, one cup of flour, half a cup of milk, and half a cup of sugar, one teaspoon of baking powder, one teaspoon of vanilla, and a tablespoon of lard. She would make that three times for three cakes. There was no way or know-how to make toppings, so she sprinkled some brown sugar on top of the cakes.

Secretly she asked Benny to find some way to get Mother out of the house so she could bake the cake. He suggested, "I will find time to clean up the barn as Mother and I always do every day, only I shall try and make it last longer."

Lea added, "I will phone Grandma while the cakes are baking."

Uncle Jack answered the phone call and promised, "I will give your grandma the message."

Lea was happy when evening came. She had supper all fixed when Helen came in.

With a delightful smile Helen exclaimed, "Yum! It sure smells good; what is it?" The children only smiled. They felt that some guests should have arrived by now. Lea had also invited the neighbors across the road. They waited and waited, but finally Lea and Benny left the table to get the cake. They sang "Happy Birthday, Mother." She was very surprised and pleased, but not one person came.

Several days later Helen mentioned to the neighbors the nice birthday surprise her children had given her. The neighbors confessed that Lea had invited them, but they had thought it was just the children's prank.

On June 1, Helen announced to her children that she would go away for a few days to get married to Mr. James Freeling. "You know, my children, he will be your father when we come back," she said.

Benny and Lea gave a loud sigh, but Rachel was happy to have more companions to play with. Then Helen also said, "The whole Freeling family will move in after next week."

After Helen left (she did not heed the unhappy faces of her three) they took a heavy blanket and huddled in the dark corner, which they had always done when their mother went away. They did not go to bed or eat until she came back. The dog sensed their emotional state and barked all night and kept running around the house. Lea was so frustrated with thoughts of the man who made her mother weep every time he came to visit and how now she was to call him her father.

Benny, Lea, and Rachel had been leading a quiet life. They had grown and developed according to their years. The open skies and wide prairie encouraged their dreams to float around. There were no crimes, murders, or violence to frighten their dreams and no churches or community activities to interfere with their own activities. They were always happy and had vigorous ambitions and were full of mischief with their own inventions. They were not aware of missing a father or needing more brothers or sisters. Their knowledge of music or stage plays came from school. Most of the teachers came from England, and their stories and plays were about kings, queens, and princesses.

Benny and Lea were old enough to realize that life would never be the same again, and this frightened and worried them extremely.

There was a lot of confusion, buzzing, and excitement while the furniture was brought in and the two families' holdings were mixed. The whole new family merged with the furniture.

The old cottage and the new house were joined by a long, unheated hallway. The girls would sleep in the small upstairs of the cottage. The parents had the bedroom that had been the living room of the cottage. The cottage kitchen was used as a catchall. The four Freeling boys and Benny had the upstairs of the new house. The main floor was a very large combined living room, kitchen, and dining room.

Chapter XX

Two Families Become One
Family—1920

In the first year the two families tried hard to adjust to their new way of living. Helen wanted her husband to take over the discipline of the family. The husband was a meek and kind person. He was more gray-haired than Lea's grandpa. His short gray beard (called a goatee) and mustache made him look like a teacher, but he was no disciplinarian. When the children asked him if they could take a walk he would answer, "Go ask Mother," so they went to ask Mother and she would say, "Go ask Father." This encouraged the children to go as they pleased.

When Mother was not around, the bigger boys would get the fiddle, harmonica, and accordion and jazz it up while the younger children would square dance or do the minuet or the Highland fling, which they had learned in school.

The parents picked up a new interest. They were influenced by the *Physical Culture Magazine*, which was about bodybuilding and toughening the body and showed pictures of people in the snow in the nude. To enter a contest with snapshots taken in the snow, Mr. Freeling insisted on making the young girls run in the snow in the nude, taking snapshots with a square brown camera and posing them in dancing position. Lea was very unsure about this and rebelled. Later she got ahold of the camera and stamped on it with both feet, smashing it flat.

Mr. Freeling was always friendly, without ambitions of his own and trying one avocation after another while evading any physically strenuous work. His favorite phrase was, "When my ship comes in I will be on Easy Street." He had many talents but was master of none; he learned everything from reading.

Every evening when the family gathered around the table, the father read short stories. His favorite stories were deathbed stories. He read the sad stories until he had all the children crying, then sent them to bed.

Helen was pregnant, and after eight years of widowhood, she found it hard to cope with. She was always nauseous during the whole nine months of her pregnancy.

One day Lea came in after school, happily skipping rope, and her stepfather came to talk to her in a very serious tone. "Your mother is ill and must take to bed. She has asked you to take over in the kitchen," he said.

The first thing Lea had to do was fetch a bucket of potatoes from the basement and peel them and cut them in small slices to fry in two large frying pans. Standing by the stove and stirring the potatoes was a heavy job for an eleven-year-old. The father would make the Postum, and the only other food was bread, butter, and milk. Sometimes chitterlings or chopped pork was added to the potatoes. Lea stood over the stove for several hours every evening after school. When she was baking the bread, she did not have enough strength to knead it. It took a lot of bread dough for twelve people. Early in the morning she would cook porridge in a six-quart kettle.

The boys sat on a long bench against the wall while the girls sat across the table on chairs. Lea's place was at the end near the stove, her mother's place.

The boys preferred their porridge served in large flat soup bowls with soup spoons. Lea dished each serving out by the stove. They spread sugar on top of the porridge and let the sugar melt, also adding a little milk on the side. Lea would stand and watch them gobble it down with much speed.

She placed her brother beside her, giving him a small bowl, and he would wait until she was settled down to eat. He was very thin and small for his age. The big boys constantly teased and bullied him. Lea still felt it her duty to mother and protect her brother.

Lea's stepfather would fix a dish to take to her mother. He would not let any of the children see her, claiming that she was always too ill to see anyone. That worried Lea and Benny.

On Mondays Lea had to stay home from school to do the family washing. The heavy woolen long underwear was almost too heavy to wring out by hand. Hanging those heavy, wet clothes on the washline in below zero weather was very strenuous. Before she had the clothespins on them, they were frozen stiff as a board. Going out from the steaming tub of water to the below zero weather caused Lea to get a sore throat. In the morning she would have a fever, which caused her to miss another day from school.

These weekly sore throats caused her to lose her voice. She could not read out loud in school and even started to spit up blood. She would be so tired after cooking dinner and cleaning up that she crawled upstairs on her knees. Her happy smiles disappeared; her rosy cheeks were no more. Her grades fell, and her stepsisters called her Dummy.

If one dish was left undone, the father would find a leather strap from the horse's harness and threaten the girls.

The dishes were washed on the eating table. One girl washed them in a large pan of hot, soapy water, the next girl rinsed them in another, and the third girl had to dry each dish. Only one plate was used per person, and a cup was used to drink water, milk, and Postum. One spoon served as fork and knife.

Father washed the frying pans. Lea did not have the strength to lift the large frying pans. Also it was noted that Lea could not scrub the floors anymore, and this left the boys to scrub the wide hardwood floorboards from then on.

Rachel and the youngest stepsister were never around. They were always out where the boys worked.

Finally the young cook got weary of peeling potatoes. She browsed around the big pantry to find some boxes from Watkins' Supplies that Mr. Freeling had not sold and started to read the instructions on them. This turned out to be powdered fruit in envelopes which said: "Add hot water." All evening Lea and her stepfather walked in and out checking whether the liquid had set, but nothing happened; they decided to check again in the morning. At five in the morning Lea found that the dessert had settled and decided to treat the family with an extra surprise for breakfast.

After their long, hard day, they all sat quietly studying or reading at the large table by a kerosene lamp placed in the center. Father came from the cottage looking very sad, with tears rolling down his cheeks and whiskers, asking each child, "Go and see Mother and say good-bye. She is on her way to heaven."

Lea looked at her mother, so still and pale. Slowly she touched her hand, then squeezed it a little harder, but there was no response.

Lea looked up at her stepfather asking, "Is she dead?"

He answered in a whisper, "Try to talk to her."

Bending over to listen to her mother's chest, she wept out loud like a heartbroken adult. Just then she felt movement on Mother's chest. Looking into her mother's face, she saw tears rolling down the face of death. She spoke out loud to her mother: "We need you. I cannot be without you any longer. Please come back."

Lea's stepfather put his arms around her and guided her out of the room.

He spoke to all the children, saying, "Mother was expecting a baby anytime, but I cannot tell if the baby is still alive."

*　*　*

It was a beautiful autumn afternoon as the children came home from school. The wheat fields were waving from the breeze, like lakes of gold, waiting for the harvest. The prairie grass was beginning to turn tan. The children stepped into the house surprised to see a tall, heavy woman holding a tiny baby who introduced herself as the midwife. Consoling the children, she said, "Your mother is doing well," and waited for the children to smile. Not one of them asked to look at the baby boy. She explained, "I will be here taking care of your mother and the baby for two weeks."

Lea was hoping that she would have some help in the house from this midwife. The next day she discovered that she must keep on peeling potatoes.

Two weeks later, the midwife brought the baby to Lea, saying, "Now I shall show you how to bathe this baby." Fearfully Lea took the baby in her arms. While the woman brought in the dishpan and set it near the kitchen stove, Lea watched very carefully.

The following day after school, Lea knew her first job was to bathe the baby. She walked into her mother's room and said, "I have come to take care of the baby," and was startled to see her mother sitting on the rocking chair nursing the baby and smiling up at her.

Lea managed to bathe the baby, and when she was pinning the diaper she struggled to get the safety pin through the heavy cloth. It slipped and stabbed the baby's stomach; he cried

145

furiously and so did Lea. Her stepfather came in to comfort Lea and swabbed the bleeding baby.

In the morning the family was surprised to see Helen working by the stove cooking the cereal. She was not much on conversation, but she and Lea worked as a team.

Now Lea was an adolescent. If she became moody, temperamental, or argumentative no one paid any attention. Her grades were improving, but she was feeling rebellious. Not wanting to be disciplined, she considered herself grown-up after having been treated like a slave at home. She convinced herself that no one had the right to tell her what to do. At this time if a young person became obnoxious enough or rebellious in a loud way, it was an excuse for a good whipping, either by the schoolteacher or parent; most of the time it was from both sides. The teenager or adolescent had no right to speak his or her own mind or explain his actions. Some young boys would leave home, even if it was to go to work on another farm. The main point was to discipline the child to break his willpower and beat him into a meek and humble character. If the young person was strong enough to take all this punishment then he usually turned out to be a good citizen. But many turned bitter toward the parents and teachers. Often years later "forgive and forget" was the policy.

One day Benny and Lea were running after a runaway horse until it reached the corral, then Lea collapsed and fainted in the yard. Her stepfather came running, carried her indoors, and put her on the couch in the parents' sitting room.

Lea came out of her blackout with her parents hovering over her. Her mother had changed her clothes and laid a heavy blanket over her. Her stepfather was talking very softly, saying, "You are now a lady, a grown-up girl, and from now on you will have this bleeding every month."

Lea was shocked and frightened by such talk. She hadn't the slightest idea what he was talking about. He went on saying,

"Times like these you must keep yourself warm and take it easy."

She was puzzled and ashamed and angrily screamed, "Why did this happen to me?"

Her mother smiled. "It happens to all girls; it will happen to the other girls upstairs. You happen to be the first one, even if you are not the oldest."

Lea retorted, "Please do not tell anyone about this." She covered her face with a pillow and gulped down sobs.

Lea did not make her appearance for breakfast, but her stepfather explained that she was not feeling well. With a constant grin he fixed a tray to take to her.

In the evening Lea went upstairs to join the girls. They asked questions such as why she was getting all the attention. Biting her lips with anger and determination, she gave no answer.

In the morning she served breakfast as usual. When she handed the dishes of cereal to the boys they said, "Thank you," instead of purposely bumping her arm.

While sweeping the floors, the boys had always stepped on the dirt and ground it into the floor; now they walked around it. When she came to the table, the boys rose to give her a chair. Instead of abusive words she heard compliments. This was all very frustrating to her.

Mr. Freeling kept talking about going to the land of sunshine—California. "The Paradise," he called it. The children did not take him seriously, as he was always saying, "When my ship comes in I will be rich." He always had some phase of special studies, and lately it had been the study of the stars. He even made his own telescope from a kit he ordered. He also spoke four languages fluently, French, German, Dutch, and English.

One day the children arrived home from school at the usual 4:30 P.M. when their mother told them, "Father has left home

147

to see what California is like." It seemed no surprise to the family. Helen had paid all his past debts and had provided enough cash for the trip.

His letters to his family came fast, two letters at a time. All he wrote about was the utopia of his dreams that had come true—the warm weather, fruit trees, and grape fields.

Helen felt he was exaggerating. He always mentioned the wine, and she realized it was the wine that was making him write so exuberantly. She worried that he had broken his promise, made on their wedding day, never to drink alcohol again. She remembered her father saying, "Once an alcoholic always an alcoholic. Even if he stops drinking for a time, it will always come back."

A fat letter came from Helen's husband ordering her to sell out and come to join him, bringing the complete family. She asked the neighbors and her brothers to help set up an auction to sell all the furniture, cattle, milking supplies, horses, chickens, pigs, buggies, sleds, and garden tools. The auction was set up to be in two weeks.

She wrote a note to the schoolteacher to have the children's report cards ready in one week and, since it was close to spring, she wanted the children promoted to the next grades.

Spending all night every night sewing dresses for the girls and herself, Helen ordered new shoes for all ten children, and suits for each boy from the Eaton catalogue of Winnipeg, Manitoba, asking them to rush the order, as she needed them in three weeks.

Helen announced, "Tomorrow is your last day in this school. Say good-bye to your friends. You will never be back." The "never be back" remark was a sudden blow in the chests of the young-hearted children. It stirred their emotional thinking and filled them with frustration and apprehension.

The five girls and two boys, with their report cards in hand, sprinted with light steps into the buggy. They started to sing,

"No more British teachers to beat us. She can go where she belongs. We do not care," waving their arms and jumping up and down. This caused the buggy to give extra bounces on the springs and frightened the two horses into a fast gallop. They continued to sing, "No more snowstorms, no wild cattle, no big prairies, and no more driving so far to school. We are going to leave. We are going to Paradise and taking a long, long ride on a train."

Only the badgers and distant coyotes could hear this screaming joy.

When they arrived home the children's voices were hoarse and the horses snorted, "We are wet with sweat."

Mother had a good dinner of fresh roast beef and mashed potatoes. She stated at the table, "This will be your last hot meal until we get to California. The neighbors will drive us to the train, and we will leave from Swalwell, then change in Lethbridge and cross the Rocky Mountains at Crowsnest Pass until we get to the border at Kingsgate. This is the plan for the trip that the agent at the depot wrote down." Each child took a turn studying the plan, but there was no map, just the words of the agent.

Mother planned the daily food for a week's traveling. Each child would have a beef sandwich and a cookie for lunch, and for dinner there would be a biscuit with boiled ham. Breakfast was a hard-boiled egg. The liquid would be water unless there was milk to be bought at the station stops. She hoped there would be apples to be bought, but had a couple of bags of dried prunes tucked away.

The children's excitement in going so far away to a land they knew nothing about could not be explained or measured. The scenery was dull, mostly prairie or wheat fields until they got closer to the mountains. They observed all the trees that had suffered from the fires which they had heard about. The forest fires in the Rockies caused the smoky air, and now they

149

saw the results. The children turned very quiet and sad about all the bare, black trees. The train was swaying and making a lot of curves, seeming as if it were moving on rocks. They were well behaved and invented their own games and did a lot of singing. The little brother who was a year old did not sleep well and cried a lot. The mountains seemed very high, with snow still on the tops. It was getting warmer as the train shook and rocked toward the south.

Close to the border town of Kingsgate, the conductor came to ask a lot of questions. Each one had to sign his or her first name. Each child signed his or her name and an initial of his or her mother's maiden name. The conductor insisted that they had to have full middle names and told them that he would give them an hour to make up middle names, which had to start with the initial of their mother's name. They all felt rushed. Lea chose the name Lottie, as she had said good-bye to her dearest friend named Lottie. She never did use the name or like it.

Getting off the train, they faced more questions by the inspectors. Helen was asked where her husband was born, and all she could say was, "He was born on a voyage across the Atlantic Ocean coming from Europe to America." They wanted the name of the ship.

"The only solution is that you and your family will have to stay until we get the name of the ship. We have no hotel on the Canadian side. You will have to go across the street to the American side, and we shall phone your husband in California for the name of the ship," she was told.

The family trailed along behind Helen as they walked over to the hotel. While Helen asked for some rooms and explained the delay, the American inspectors had a good laugh. The family was assigned to several bedrooms and a large parlor. For several days everything went smoothly. Helen marched to the Canadian office every afternoon expecting an answer from her husband. Three times he answered the telegram with: "I don't

150

know; no record was made." The Canadians kept repeating the question every day until Mr. Freeling decided to make up a name. By this time a week had already gone by. The food was all gone, and the children were hungry. Helen had plenty of money sewed in the hem of her skirt, but the American side of this town had the food stores, the restaurants, and the one hotel and they would not accept Canadian money. Since Mother was nursing the baby, at least he was not going hungry.

The young people spent a lot of time outdoors taking walks into the deep woods to look for berries. This was a beautiful area in terms of the landscape, with mountains all around.

A telegram finally reached the American border patrol with the name of the ship Mr. Freeling guessed was the one.

By noon the family was packed up to board the train. The American station exchanged all the Canadian money that Helen was carrying into American. The train had no dining room, so food had to be bought before boarding the train.

By evening the children were contented and happy, with their stomachs full. They had a lot of laughs watching a fat woman walking back and forth to throw eggshells into the wastebasket. She was constantly eating hard-boiled eggs from a large basketful beside her. She wobbled and hit every seat with her hip, scolding at each bump. "The train makes so much noise that I can hardly walk!" she exclaimed. The young people watched with their mouths open with amazement to see her eat so many hard-boiled eggs and then, with her apron full of shells, wobble like a big duck to the wastebasket and back.

On hearing the announcement of approaching California, the children acted like they were glued to the windows to get sight of the Paradise they had heard so much about. They were to get off the train in Fresno, and all they could see for miles and miles was sand. The conductor told them that soon they would come to rows and rows of grape plants and they would

On the train looking over the landscape of California—1923

see peach trees. It was all very flat with no hills until they gazed out to the east and saw the High Sierras.

Lea had been very quiet and calm. She felt frustrated and sad and wondered what would be ahead for her. One thing she was certain of was that life would never be the same again, for which she was glad.

This San Joaquin Valley was as flat as the prairie country, but all sand instead of grass. In 1923 California seemed like a new, young country, with only a few hard-surfaced roads.

As they departed from the train, the faces, clothes and houses and even the air and sun looked different.